FINANCIAL LITERACY FOR KIDS, SIMPLIFIED!

EQUIPPING PARENTS TO EASILY TEACH THEIR KIDS FUN AND EFFECTIVE MONEY MANAGEMENT SKILLS AND STRATEGIES ON: SAVING, INVESTING, AND BUDGETING!

MAX MILES

I would like to express my heartfelt gratitude to my sister, Lisa Simone, for her invaluable support throughout the creation of this book. Her willingness to engage with my ideas and her patience in listening to my calls day and night were crucial in shaping the content. Without her insights and encouragement, this book would not have reached completion.

This work is dedicated to my dear son, Evan. Every page, every word, and every thought reflects the boundless love and joy he brings into my life. From the moment I held him in my arms to the laughter we share and the quiet moments we spend reading together, he inspires me to be the best father I can be.

May this book serve as a small token of my love for him, a legacy for the future, and a cherished reminder of the precious moments we share.

The best time to plant a tree was twenty years ago.

The second best time is now.

— CHINESE PROVERB

TABLE OF CONTENTS

INTRODUCTION

Let me tell you about a moment that sparked a revelation for me. I was at the grocery store with my young niece, and she was eyeing a shiny toy displayed at the checkout. She asked if she could have it, and I told her she could save up for it. Her puzzled look made me realize she had no clue about saving money. Right there, it hit me how crucial it is to introduce money concepts to kids early on. Helping them understand the basics of saving, spending, and making smart choices can set them up for a lifetime of financial well-being.

Welcome to *Financial Literacy for Kids, Simplified!* This book empowers you and your children to make informed financial decisions. My vision is to simplify complex financial topics, making them accessible and enjoyable for young minds. By breaking down these concepts, we aim to make learning about money an exciting adventure rather than a daunting task.

The purpose of this book is simple: to bridge the gap between your financial knowledge and your ability to teach it to your kids. I aim to cultivate lifelong financial habits through interactive and fun learning methods. Money doesn't have to be a mystery or something to fear. It can be part of everyday life, something your children understand and manage confidently.

We'll cover critical topics such as saving, investing, budgeting, and understanding the difference between needs and wants. These are simplified through engaging lessons that resonate with children. Imagine your child understanding how to budget their weekly allowance or save up for something special they want. It's all about making these concepts relatable and easy to grasp.

The book includes interactive activities, illustrations, stories, and examples to make these lessons stick. These elements are designed to engage your child and help them apply what they learn in real-life situations. Whether it's a game that teaches saving or a story about a young investor, these activities make learning about money fun and memorable.

This book is for you, whether you're a parent or a single parent with children aged 8 to 12. I understand how busy life can be and how finding time for financial education can seem challenging. That's why "*Financial Literacy for Kids, Simplified!*" is crafted to be practical and time-efficient, fitting seamlessly into your daily routine.

Let me share a bit about what drives me. My parents were financially savvy, yet they had not explicitly shared those principles with me. Later in life, I realized how valuable those lessons could have been. This experience fuels my dedication to helping parents like you provide their children with a solid financial foundation. I want to ensure that kids today have access to the knowledge that can lead them toward financial freedom.

The expected outcome for you and your children is a positive money mindset that lasts for years. By using the tools in this book, your child will be able to confidently navigate their financial future. You'll see them make wise money choices and develop habits that will benefit them.

So, I invite you to start this financial education journey with your children. Together, we can make learning about money a rewarding and enjoyable experience. Let's turn what might seem daunting into a fun adventure that empowers your kids and sets them on a path to financial success.

1

THE BASICS OF MONEY

One Saturday morning, I overheard a conversation between two kids at a local park. One was bragging about how many toys he had, while the other seemed puzzled, asking, "How do you get so many toys?" The first one replied, "I just ask my parents!" This simple exchange got me thinking about how our children perceive money and how crucial it is to teach them its value. Understanding money isn't just about knowing how to spend it; it's about learning its role in our lives. It can be a magical tool when used wisely, yet it can also be a source of confusion if misunderstood. So, as we explore the basics of money, we'll make these concepts as clear and relatable as possible, ensuring they become a natural part of your child's everyday thinking.

WHAT IS MONEY? UNDERSTANDING ITS VALUE

Money is more than just coins and bills; it's a tool that helps us exchange things of value. Imagine money as a bridge connecting our necessities with what we want or need. It acts as a medium, a common ground where value can be traded without the hassle of bartering items like apples or oranges. This common currency allows us to buy goods and services, like groceries or haircuts, making transactions smoother and more straightforward. When children understand this, they start to see money as a facilitator rather than just an object. It's what we use daily to make purchases, exchange for goods like toys or snacks, and services like music lessons or a trip to the zoo.

To help children grasp the value of money, we can compare the costs of everyday items. For instance, a new toy might cost as much as 10 candy bars. This comparison helps them understand that money is exchanged for value and that value varies depending on the item. The cost of something often reflects its scarcity and demand. For example, a rare collector's card might be more expensive than a common one simply because fewer are available, and more people want it. This scarcity principle teaches children why some things are more valuable than others. It's like understanding why a limited-edition game is pricier than a regular edition. When kids begin to appreciate this, they start seeing money's role in determining value.

Interactive Activity: Classroom Marketplace

Let's make this learning fun and interactive. Set up a classroom marketplace where each child has a small amount of pretend money. Lay out various items, each with a price tag, such as pencils, stickers, and small toys. Encourage the children to decide what they'd like to "purchase" and why. This activity reinforces the idea of money as a medium of exchange. It gives them a sense of decision-making based on value. Watch as they weigh their options, perhaps opting for a slightly pricier item that they value more. Through this playful simulation, they learn firsthand how money works in transactions and how value is determined by what they consider important. This simple exercise can spark a deeper understanding and appreciation of money's role in our lives.

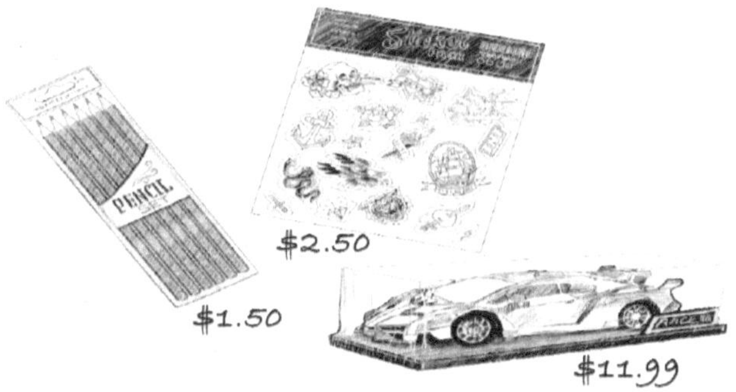

A decision-making exercise to help kids weigh value of items, questioning what they would like to purchase and why.

By engaging children in such activities, we teach them about money and empower them to make informed decisions. As they navigate through choices and see the consequences of their spending, they begin to develop a sense of financial responsibility. This foundational knowledge is crucial as it sets the stage for more complex financial concepts they'll encounter as they grow. Through these experiences, children start to see money as something to be spent and a tool that requires thoughtful management. It plants the seeds for financial literacy that will benefit them for a lifetime.

THE HISTORY OF MONEY: FROM BARTER TO DIGITAL

A farmer bartering fruits & vegetables with a baker for her freshly baked loaves of bread.

Imagine a time when there was no money, and people relied on trading goods directly. This was the era of bartering, where people exchanged what they had for what they needed. Picture a farmer with a basket of fruits and vegetables, looking to trade with a baker for bread. The farmer was out of luck if the baker didn't need fruits or vegetables. This system had its limitations. It required a mutual need, which was sometimes challenging to find. For instance, if you had a goat but needed shoes, you'd have to find someone who needed a goat and had extra shoes to spare.

This inefficiency led to the creation of money, making transactions simpler and more universal.

As societies grew, so did the need for a more efficient system of trade. Enter coins, a game-changer in the world of exchange. Coins made of metals like gold and silver began circulating around 600 BC in places like Ancient Turkey. These coins, often stamped with the images of rulers, were durable and widely accepted. In Roman times, coins became a staple of daily transactions, allowing people to easily buy goods and pay taxes. Paper money came later, first appearing in China around the seventh century. Unlike heavy coins, paper money was easy to carry and could represent more significant sums. By the 1600s, Europe adopted banknotes, further simplifying trade and commerce.

Ancient coins from Egypt, Rome and Turkey.

Fast forward to today, where digital currency has transformed how we think about money. With the click of a button, you can transfer money or pay for services using debit cards and mobile apps. This shift to digital forms of money reflects our increasingly interconnected world. Digital transactions eliminate the need for physical cash and provide convenience and security. Imagine buying a book online and paying with a card number instead of handing over bills. This digital age opens up new ways for children to learn about money, preparing them for a future where cash might be less familiar.

The story of the first minted coins is fascinating, illustrating how necessity drives innovation. The Kingdom of Lydia, located in what is now Turkey, is credited with creating the first standardized coins around 600 BC. These coins were stamped from a mixture of gold and silver called electrum and featured images representing the kingdom. This innovation was not just about making trade easier but a leap toward creating a unified economic system. Coins allowed for more complex economies and laid the groundwork for today's currencies. They symbolized trust and acceptance, something that mere barter could never achieve.

These historical developments show a progression from simple trades to sophisticated systems that manage vast economies. Money has evolved from tangible items to digital transactions, making our lives more convenient. As parents, sharing these stories with your children can spark curiosity and help them appreciate the countless efforts that brought us to this point. By understanding where money comes from, kids can better grasp its value and role in our lives. This context enriches their financial literacy, making them more informed as they navigate their financial futures.

EARNING MONEY: CHORES, ALLOWANCES, AND MORE

Imagine a bustling Saturday morning at home. The sun streams through the windows as you and your child set the table for breakfast. It's a perfect time to introduce the concept of earning money by doing chores. Washing dishes, tidying their room, or even helping with the garden can all become opportunities for children to learn the value of work. These tasks, though simple, teach them responsibility and the satisfaction of a job well done. Children start to see the connection between effort and reward by associating chores with earning. It's like a mini economy right in your home, where they can begin to understand that money doesn't just magically appear; it's earned through hard work and dedication.

Allowances can be a valuable tool in this learning process. Setting up a weekly allowance system tied to the completion of chores provides a structured way for children to manage their earnings. It's not just about handing out money; it's about teaching budgeting and saving. Consider establishing a chart where each completed task earns a specific amount. At the end of the week, they receive their earnings.

This system helps them learn to prioritize tasks and manage their time, all while getting a taste of financial independence. They can decide whether to save for a larger goal or spend on tiny treats, learning firsthand the consequences of their financial decisions. This process instills a sense of accomplishment and sets the groundwork for future financial literacy.

Beyond chores and allowances, there are other creative ways children can earn money, fostering a spirit of entrepreneurship. Setting up a lemonade stand on a warm summer day, for instance, or organizing a garage sale with old toys and books can be exciting. These endeavors teach children the basics of running a small business, from handling money to interacting with customers. They learn to set prices, manage change, and market their stand with homemade signs. Such experiences are invaluable, offering practical lessons in financial management, communication, and creativity. By encouraging these activities, you nurture a sense of initiative and problem-solving, which will serve them well in any future endeavor.

Role-Playing Scenario: The Home Economy

Create a role-playing scenario where your child can simulate earning and spending money. Set up a pretend chore and payment system at home. Assign various tasks, each with a designated value, and give your child play money to manage. They can earn money by completing tasks like vacuuming the living room, folding laundry, or washing dishes.

Children earning money by completing chores

Once they've earned enough, let them "spend" it on fun activities, like extra screen time or a special treat. This role-playing game makes learning about earning and spending interactive and engaging. It allows children to practice decision-making in a safe environment. It's a tangible way for them to experience the dynamics of earning money while understanding its value. Through this playful approach, children become more confident and capable of handling money, preparing them for real-world financial situations.

These experiences enrich your child's understanding of money and empower them to take charge of their financial journey. They learn that money is something to be spent and a tool to use wisely. They develop essential life skills beyond financial literacy by earning through chores, receiving allowances, or starting small ventures. This foundation of knowledge and experience equips them with the ability to make informed decisions, set goals, and understand the value of their efforts. As they grow, these lessons will be instrumental in shaping their financial habits and setting them on a path to success.

NEEDS VS. WANTS: MAKING SMART CHOICES

Picture this: It's a sunny afternoon, and you and your child are at the mall. You've just finished buying new shoes, and suddenly, you hear, "Can I get that toy?" This moment is the perfect opportunity to introduce one of the most fundamental concepts in financial literacy: distinguishing between needs and wants. Needs are the essentials we can't do without—like food, clothing, and a safe place to live. They are the building blocks of everyday life, ensuring we have what we require to survive and thrive.

Conversely, wants are the extras—those delightful things that bring joy but aren't necessary for our well-being. Toys, candy, and the latest gadgets fall into this category. By teaching children to differentiate between the two, we equip them with the skills to make informed decisions and prioritize spending.

Let's take it a step further by encouraging thoughtful decision-making. Imagine using a decision-making flowchart. Start with a simple question: "Do I need this?" If the answer is yes, it's likely a need. If no, ask, "Do I want this more than something else I might buy later?" This approach helps children assess their choices and fosters patience and critical thinking. It's like giving them a roadmap to navigate their desires, teaching them to weigh options and consider consequences. Over time, this habit of evaluation becomes second nature, guiding them through more complex financial decisions as they grow.

Real-life scenarios serve as excellent teaching tools. Consider the situation where a child has to choose between buying a toy now or saving for an exciting school trip. It's a tangible way for them to see the impact of their decisions. By discussing the pros and cons of each choice, parents can guide their children through the thought process involved. Do they want immediate gratification with the toy, or do they value the experience and memories that the trip promises? These discussions educate and empower children to take ownership of their decisions, instilling a sense of responsibility and foresight.

Interactive Discussion Activity: Needs vs. Wants Collage

Try engaging your child with a needs versus wants collage activity. Gather old magazines, scissors, glue, and a large piece of paper. Encourage your child to cut out pictures representing needs and wants. They can paste images of necessities like fruits, vegetables, and school supplies on one side of the paper. Conversely, they can place pictures of things they desire, like video games or comics. This visual representation helps solidify their understanding, making it easier to identify and categorize their preferences. It's a creative way to reinforce the lesson, providing a platform for discussion and reflection.

Needs versus want's collage activity

Through these exercises and conversations, children understand that not all purchases hold the same weight. They learn to appreciate the value of money and the benefits of prioritizing needs over wants. This understanding lays the groundwork for future financial literacy, preparing them to manage their resources wisely. As they grow and their financial responsibilities increase, distinguishing between needs and wants becomes crucial, influencing everything from budgeting to long-term financial planning. It's about planting seeds to become intelligent financial habits, ensuring a secure and stable future.

THE PIGGY BANK ADVENTURE: A FUN SAVING STORY

Once upon a time, a little boy named Timmy dreamed of owning a shiny red bicycle. Every day, he watched the neighborhood kids zoom past on their bikes, their laughter echoing through the street. Timmy yearned to join them, but he knew that his dream bicycle wouldn't just appear out of thin air. So, with determination in his heart, he decided to save up for it. Armed with his trusty piggy bank, Timmy embarked on a mission to turn his dream into a reality. His supportive yet firm parents explained the importance of saving and how each coin dropped into the piggy bank brought him closer to his goal.

Timmy's journey was not without temptation. On weekends, his friends would invite him to the ice cream truck, and the allure of a cold treat on a hot day was hard to resist. But Timmy had a plan. He saved half his weekly allowance and any extra money from helping with chores. It was challenging. There were days when he wanted to spend on small toys or treats, but each time, he'd pause and say to himself, "Bicycle first, then fun." This mantra guided him, and slowly, he watched his piggy bank grow heavier with savings.

As weeks turned into months, Timmy faced a critical decision. He had saved enough to buy a smaller, less fancy bike or continue saving for his dream one. Timmy's parents encouraged him to hold out for the red bicycle. This lesson in delayed gratification taught him the value of patience and perseverance. Saving, he realized, was like planting seeds and waiting for them to sprout. It required time, care, and sometimes a little sacrifice, but the rewards were worth it.

Jimmy with his trusty piggy bank is on a mission to purchase his dream bicycle

Interactive elements can make this story even more engaging for children. Imagine asking your child what they would do in Timmy's situation. Would they buy the smaller bike or continue saving? How would they handle the temptation of treats and toys? These questions make the story interactive and help children empathize with Timmy's choices, encouraging them to think critically about their own financial decisions.

Finally, the day arrived when Timmy had saved enough to buy the bicycle of his dreams. The moment he handed his carefully saved money to the bike store assistant and felt the smooth handlebars of his new bike was one of triumph and fulfillment. His hard work and dedication had paid off. Timmy's story teaches us that saving is not just about accumulating money; it's about discipline, foresight, and the joy of achieving a well-earned goal.

The moral of Timmy's tale is clear: Saving leads to achieving goals and reaping rewards. Understanding this concept early on can shape children's approach to money for years to come. As parents, fostering this mindset is crucial. It's about more than just teaching them to save; it's about instilling values that will guide them throughout life. Timmy's adventure with his piggy bank becomes a metaphor for the broader journey of financial responsibility, a journey each child can embark on with the proper guidance and encouragement.

As we close this chapter, remember that the stories and lessons we share with our children today lay the groundwork for their financial future. By nurturing their understanding of saving and spending, we empower them to make choices that reflect wisdom and joy. It's not just about filling a piggy bank; it's about filling their lives with the knowledge and skills to help them thrive.

2

SMART SAVING HABITS

Imagine your child staring at a colorful jigsaw puzzle, eager to see the whole picture but knowing it takes patience and strategy. Saving money is much like that puzzle; each piece represents a small step toward a larger goal. It's about teaching kids that their dreams, whether a new book or an exciting school trip, can become reality with the right approach. Saving isn't just about stashing away coins; it's an essential life skill that empowers them to plan and prioritize, turning abstract desires into tangible achievements. With each coin saved, they get closer to seeing the complete picture of their goal, much like fitting together those final pieces of the puzzle.

Saving for a specific goal, like a desired toy or a book, introduces children to delayed gratification. It teaches them that by holding off on more minor, immediate pleasures, they can work toward something more rewarding in the Future. For instance, if your child is eyeing a toy that costs 10 dollars, they can learn to save a portion of their allowance each week until they reach the total amount. This process builds discipline and instills a sense of accomplishment once the goal is achieved. The look of pride on their face when they finally hold that toy is priceless, a testament to their patience and planning. The satisfaction comes from knowing they worked hard for something they truly wanted. This exercise in saving becomes a powerful lesson in managing resources and making thoughtful choices.

Long-term goals offer a broader perspective, like saving for a school trip or even a bicycle. They require more time, effort, and planning, showing children the value of persistence. These goals might seem overwhelming initially, but breaking them down into smaller, manageable steps makes them achievable. A child might set aside a little monthly money for a year to afford that trip. This teaches them about commitment and the importance of sticking to a plan. It's like planting a tree and watching it grow over time, with sunlight and water contributing to its eventual height each day. Through this process, children learn that big dreams often require significant effort, and the rewards are even sweeter when earned through perseverance. This understanding lays the foundation for financial habits that will benefit them throughout their lives.

The difference between short-term and long-term goals is crucial. Short-term goals, like saving for a video game, are within immediate reach and provide quick satisfaction. They teach children about setting priorities and making choices. On the other hand, long-term goals, such as saving for a bicycle, require more planning and patience. They help children develop foresight and strategic thinking, invaluable skills as they mature. By learning to juggle both types of goals, kids become adept at managing their resources and time. This balance is essential, as it mirrors the complexity of real-life financial planning, where individuals must often decide between instant gratification and future security. By mastering this balance, children are better prepared to handle the economic challenges they will face as adults.

Visual Activity: Creating a Vision Board for Savings Goals

Consider creating a vision board with your child to make the process more engaging. Gather magazines, scissors, glue, and a poster board. Encourage your child to cut out images of their goals—a toy, book, or even a future trip—and paste them on the board. This visual representation is a daily reminder of what they're working toward, keeping them motivated to save. It transforms the abstract concept of saving into something concrete and inspiring. Each image on the board represents a piece of their financial puzzle, and as their savings grow, they can watch their dreams take shape. This activity makes goal-setting fun and tangible, providing a constant source of inspiration and direction.

As parents, guiding children through these steps is a rewarding experience. It's not just about teaching them to save money; it's about empowering them to take control of their financial future. By instilling the habit of saving from an early age, you give them the tools to navigate life's financial challenges confidently and efficiently. They learn that with patience and planning, they can achieve their dreams and that the journey to get there is just as important as the destination. Through saving, they discover the power of setting goals, making informed choices, and ultimately, realizing their potential.

Vision Board

MEET YOUR BUDGET BUDDY: HOW TO TRACK SAVINGS

Imagine the excitement of setting up a lemonade stand on a sunny day, with your child eagerly counting each coin that drops into their jar. But what happens when they want to know how much they've saved up for that new game or special outing? This is where the concept of budgeting comes in, acting as a roadmap for their financial adventures. Budgeting is all about understanding how much money comes in and how much goes out. It's a tool that helps track savings and spending, ensuring every penny has a purpose. For kids, a simple budgeting chart can transform abstract numbers into a visual story, where each line represents a step closer to their goals. This chart can be as straightforward as three columns labeled "Income," "Spending," and "Savings," quickly filled out with their weekly allowance or earnings from small chores. These charts make budgeting tangible and relatable, showing children that money management is a skill they can master.

Enter the Budget Buddy, a fictional character who becomes a child's financial companion. The Budget Buddy is a fun and friendly guide, reminding them about the importance of saving and helping them monitor their finances. Think of it as a playful sidekick who offers tips and encouragement along the way. This character can take many forms—a stuffed animal, a colorful chart, or even an app with quirky animations. The Budget Buddy helps children remember to set aside money for saving before spending, turning budgeting into a game rather than a chore. With its friendly reminders and cheerful personality, the Budget Buddy makes financial tracking a delightful part of their routine. It's like having a friend who cheers them on as they inch closer to their financial goals, one coin at a time.

Income	Saving	Spending
Allowance from Mom & Dad $30	$45	$8 on marker set
Income from Chores $15		

The Budget Buddy helps children remember to set aside money for saving before spending

Digital tools can make tracking savings even more engaging for those tech-savvy kids. A simple notebook is always handy, but utilizing apps designed for children can bring budgeting to life. These apps often feature interactive elements like goal trackers and colorful graphs, making it easier for kids to visualize their progress. With just a few taps, they can enter their earnings and see how their savings grow. The app might have features like setting alerts for reaching certain milestones or congratulatory messages when they hit savings targets. This digital approach keeps them engaged and introduces them to the world of modern finance, where digital transactions are commonplace. Children can develop a sense of responsibility and autonomy in managing their money using these tools.

Interactive Budgeting Exercise: Budgeting a Monthly Allowance

Here's a fun exercise to try:

1. Sit down with your child and work together to create a budget for their monthly allowance.
2. Start by discussing their income—perhaps it's a weekly chore allowance or money from helping out in the neighborhood.
3. Brainstorm a list of things they want to spend on, like snacks, toys, or saving for a more significant purchase.
4. Use a chart to allocate portions of their allowance into different categories.
5. Please encourage them to think about how much they want to save and what they're willing to spend.

This exercise teaches them not only about setting limits but also about making choices and prioritizing needs over wants. It's a practical lesson in money management that can be educational and fun.

Mom and kids going over budget.

Engaging in these exercises solidifies their understanding of budgeting. It fosters a sense of accomplishment as they see their savings grow. The Budget Buddy and these practical tools empower children to take charge of their financial journey, making budgeting a natural and enjoyable part of their lives. As they build these habits, they gain confidence in handling money, ensuring they're well-prepared for financial responsibilities.

SAVE, SPEND, SHARE: THE MONEY JAR METHOD

Imagine a rainbow of jars lined up on a child's shelf, each holding the promise of a lesson about money. This is the essence of the Money Jar Method, a simple yet effective way to help kids manage their finances. By dividing money into jars labeled for saving, spending, and sharing, children can visually and tangibly understand how to allocate their resources. Each jar has its purpose: to teach kids about balancing immediate desires with future goals and the joy of giving.

The saving jar is where dreams take root. It's the place for money earmarked for future goals, whether a new toy, a book, or even a more significant aspiration like a bicycle. This jar teaches patience and discipline, showing kids that saving over time can lead to achieving the things they genuinely want. It's a lesson in delayed gratification, where the anticipation of reaching a goal becomes a powerful motivator. Watching the saving jar fill up reinforces the value of careful planning and persistence.

On the other hand, the spending jar is all about the here and now. It's for immediate needs or wants, those small treats that bring smiles and instant joy. This jar allows children to enjoy their money in the present, teaching them to decide what they value. It's an exercise in budgeting, where they learn to weigh the cost of a candy bar against a trip to the arcade. Through this jar, kids understand that while it's okay to enjoy their money, it's essential to do so wisely.

Then there's the sharing jar, a symbol of generosity and empathy. This jar is for donations or gifts, teaching children the importance of giving back. Whether contributing to a local charity or buying a birthday present for a friend, the sharing jar fosters community and kindness. It helps kids see beyond their needs, encouraging them to consider how they can make a difference in someone else's life. This habit of sharing builds character and enriches their understanding of money's potential to bring joy to others.

Creating these jars can be a fun, hands-on activity that engages children and sparks their creativity. Please give them empty jars, labels, and stickers, and let them decorate each. Please encourage them to personalize the jars with drawings or colors representing their goals and values. This activity makes the concept more tangible and invests them emotionally in the process. As they decorate, they talk about what each jar means and how they might allocate their money. It's an opportunity to discuss their hopes and priorities, fostering open dialogue about financial decision-making.

Money Jars

Facilitating family discussions about how money is divided among the jars can enlighten everyone. Gather around the table and discuss your experiences with saving, spending, and sharing. Please encourage your child to share their thoughts on how and why they'd like to distribute their money. These conversations can lead to valuable insights and shared learning moments. Discussing the choices they make with their money jars allows them to reflect on their decisions and understand the impact of their financial habits. It's a way to support and guide them as they navigate the complexities of money management, building a foundation of trust and communication.

THE STORY OF PENNY THE PIGGY BANK

Once upon a time, there was a cheerful little piggy bank named Penny. Penny wasn't just any piggy bank; she was special. Her bright pink ceramic body sparkled in the sunlight, and she had a big, friendly smile that promised adventure. Penny lived on the shelf in the room of a young boy named Max. When Max receives Penny as a gift, she becomes his trusted companion in learning about money. Penny's greatest joy was helping Max save something he dearly wanted—a magnificent LEGO castle set. Max's eyes lit up whenever he talked about that castle, and Penny was determined to see him achieve his dream.

Max Thinking about a Lego Castle

As Max started saving, Penny was right there, day after day, patiently watching over the coins Max dropped into her slot. But saving wasn't always easy. The world was full of tempting things, like the sweet aroma of freshly baked cookies at the bakery or the dazzling array of toys at the local store. Max often found himself torn between the immediate thrill of spending and the promise of the castle. Penny, in her silent way, reminded Max of the joy that awaited him if he persevered. She symbolized patience and determination, teaching Max that good things come to those who wait. With each coin that rattled inside her, Penny whispered a silent cheer, encouraging Max to stay focused on his goal.

Penny's adventure wasn't without its challenges. Max's friends invited him to the amusement park one day, and the excitement was palpable. They talked about the roller coasters, the cotton candy, and the games with enticing prizes. Max's heart raced with the desire to join them, but he knew spending his savings would set him back from his castle goal. Penny seemed to wink at him from her perch, reminding him of the castle they were building together, coin by coin. At that moment, Max faced a choice: spend his savings on a fun day or keep adding to his dream. Max chose to save with a heavy but determined heart, understanding that the castle held a special place in his dreams.

Interactive storytelling can make Penny's tale even more engaging. Imagine asking your child what they would do in Max's shoes. Would they choose the amusement park or stick with Penny's plan? What advice might they give to Max? These questions encourage children to actively participate in the story, fostering empathy and critical thinking. They learn that every financial decision involves weighing options and considering future impacts. Penny's story becomes a guide, helping children navigate their financial choices confidently and clearly.

In the end, Max's dedication paid off. The day came when he finally had enough to buy the LEGO castle. Max felt a sense of pride and accomplishment as he poured out the coins from Penny's belly. The journey had taught him about the power of saving, the importance of patience, and the rewards of perseverance. Penny had been more than just a piggy bank; she was a teacher, a friend, and a reminder that dreams could come true. The castle, majestic in its entirety, stood as a testament to what Max and Penny had achieved together. The moral of Penny's story is crystal clear: Saving is not just about putting money aside; it's about building dreams, one coin at a time.

saving is not just about putting money aside
it's about building dreams one coin at a time

SETTING FINANCIAL GOALS: PLANNING FOR THE FUTURE

Imagine your child standing in front of a towering shelf in the toy store, eyes wide with excitement. They spot a toy they've been dreaming about, but it's just out of reach financially. This moment is a golden opportunity to introduce the concept of setting financial goals. Teaching kids to set goals is like giving them a map to navigate their financial future. It helps them understand that while they might not be able to buy everything they want right now, with a plan, they can work toward those desires. Clear financial goals are crucial because they give children a sense of direction and purpose in managing their money. It empowers them to make choices that align with their ambitions, whether saving for a new bicycle or planning a memorable family outing.

To set practical goals, children can learn to use the SMART technique. This approach helps them create Specific, Measurable, Achievable, Relevant, and Time-bound goals. Let's break it down: a goal should be specific, like saving for a pair of roller skates rather than just "something fun." It should be measurable, with a precise amount of money to save. Achievable means it's within their reach, so keeping a few dollars monthly might be more realistic than aiming for hundreds. The goal should be relevant to their interests, perhaps linked to a hobby or passion. And finally, it should be time-bound, with a deadline to motivate them. This structured method transforms vague wishes into actionable plans, making the process both manageable and rewarding.

To bring these concepts to life, consider incorporating planning activities that help children visualize their path to success. Creating a savings timeline can be a fun and practical tool. Grab some colorful markers and a large sheet of paper and draw a simple calendar. Please encourage your child to mark their financial goal at the end of a set period, such as three months. Then, work backward to plan how much they need to save each week to reach that goal. This visual representation turns an abstract idea into a tangible plan, allowing them to track their progress and adjust as needed. It's like watching a countdown to a special event, with each savings milestone bringing them closer to their dream. This activity teaches discipline and planning and builds excitement and anticipation as they see their goal becoming a reality.

Sharing success stories can be a powerful motivator for children. Imagine telling them about another young saver, Tamika, who set a goal to fund a family vacation. Tamika began by saving birthday money and doing extra chores, slowly building their savings over a year. When Tamika's family finally went on their trip, her contribution made it all the more remarkable, knowing she played a small part in making it happen. Or consider the story of Thomas, a budding artist who saved for art supplies, eventually creating a masterpiece that was displayed at his school's art exhibit. These stories illustrate that with determination and planning, goals can be achieved, and dreams can become reality. They inspire children to believe in their potential and understand that hard work and patience pay off.

Thomas the budding artist saved up for his art supplies.

Helping children set financial goals is about more than money; it teaches them valuable life skills. It's about instilling confidence and showing them that they have the power to shape their own future. As they learn to set and achieve goals, they gain a sense of autonomy and accomplishment. They begin to understand that, while they may face challenges, they have the tools to overcome them. By guiding your child through this process, you're not just teaching them about finances; you're equipping them with the skills they need to succeed in all areas of life. They learn that anything is possible with a clear vision, a solid plan, and the right mindset.

THE MAGIC OF COMPOUND INTEREST EXPLAINED

Imagine planting a tiny seed in your backyard, watering it regularly, and watching it grow into a tall, sturdy tree over time. This is a bit like compound interest, where your money grows as if it's gaining strength from the sun and rain. Compound interest is powerful because it allows savings to grow exponentially, not just linearly. The idea is simple: You earn interest not only on your initial savings but also on the accumulating interest. This means your money can grow faster and more substantially over time. It's like a snowball rolling down a hill, gathering more snow and increasing size. Children grasp this idea and see saving as a dynamic and rewarding process rather than just setting money aside.

This is a bit like compound interest, where your money grows as if it's gaining strength from the sun and rain.

The Tale of Mina and the Magical Money Tree

To make compound interest relatable, here is a story you can share with your kids: Once upon a time, in a sunny little village, a curious girl named Mina loved playing in her backyard. One day, while wandering, she stumbled upon a peculiar seed that shimmered in the sunlight. Without hesitation, Mina planted the seed next to her favorite apple tree.

Mina watered the seed daily and watched as it sprouted into a tiny, vibrant sapling. The sapling grew taller and more muscular each week, its branches reaching out just like the apple tree. Mina was amazed and called it her

"Money Tree" because it seemed magical, increasing, and robust.

As Mina continued her care each month, the Money Tree did something extraordinary. It sprouted shiny, golden leaves that she could pick and place in her piggy bank. These golden leaves didn't only come once, though. Every month, new leaves appeared and were even more than the last batch! Mina was delighted, watching her piggy bank grow heavier.

One day, her wise grandfather came by as Mina sat counting her golden leaves. "Oh, Mina," he chuckled, "you've discovered the secret of compound interest."

"Compound interest?" Mina repeated with a puzzled look.

Grandfather nodded. "Yes! Your Money Tree is like saving and growing money with compound interest. Just as you earned golden leaves on your original leaves, when you save money, you earn interest not just once but on your saved money and the interest it earns each time."

Mina listened closely. "So, if I save my golden leaves and wait, I can collect even more leaves next time?"

"Exactly!" Grandfather smiled. "The earlier you start saving, the bigger your Money Tree—and your golden leaves—will grow!"

Over time, Mina shared her secret with her friends, explaining how their piggy banks could grow tall and strong like her Money Tree with just a little patience and care. Together, they imagined their small piles of coins and leaves turning into tall, flourishing trees.

Oh Mina you have discovered the secret of compound interest.

And so, Mina and her friends learned the magic of compound interest, realizing their small savings could eventually turn into something grand. It was a lesson they cherished, understanding that with patience and consistent saving, their financial future could be as bright as Mina's magical Money Tree. In this story, Mina and her friends discovered not just the secret of growing their savings but a valuable lesson in patience and planning for their future!

To explain compound interest to a child, you can turn it into a fun activity. Start with a piggy bank and tell your child that every time they add $10, the piggy bank will magically add a little extra, like a bonus. If they add $10 at the end of the month, and the piggy bank adds 10% as a reward, $1 more is added, making the total $11. This is what earning interest means—the money grows on its own!

Please encourage them to imagine this happening every month when they save a set amount and earn a small percentage as a bonus. Ask them to think about how much they would have after a year of saving like this. You can use play money or a simple calculator to help them see how their savings grow month by month. This way, it becomes like a fun math game where they discover how saving a little now can lead to a bigger reward later. It's like solving a puzzle and finding a treasure at the end, showing them the magic of starting to save early and watching their money grow over time!

Starting early is critical to maximizing the benefits of compound interest. Imagine two children: one begins saving at age six, and the other waits until age ten. Even if they both save the same amount each year, the child who started earlier will have more saved up by the time they're teenagers. This early start gives compound interest more time to work magic, leading to more significant growth. It's a lesson in the power of time and patience, showing children that the sooner they start saving, the more they can benefit from compound interest. This understanding encourages them to think long-term and recognize the value of steady, consistent saving. It's like planting that seed early, giving it plenty of time to grow into a magnificent tree, providing shade and fruit for years.

As we wrap up this chapter on smart saving habits, remember that teaching children about money is more than just dollars and cents. It's about instilling values and habits to serve them well throughout their lives. From setting goals and tracking savings to understanding the magic of compound interest, these lessons empower them to make informed decisions. As we move forward, we'll explore the world of spending wisely, diving into topics that help children make wise choices in their financial lives.

3

SPENDING WISELY

On a bright Saturday afternoon, you find yourself at the grocery store with your child, weaving through the aisles as they eagerly point out every colorful cereal box and candy display that catches their eye. The familiar scene presents a perfect chance to teach them an essential lesson about intelligent shopping and financial responsibility. This chapter is about transforming those everyday shopping trips into valuable learning experiences. By guiding your child through differentiating needs from wants, you give them the tools to make thoughtful decisions that will serve them well in the future. Navigating the store together is an opportunity to instill a sense of financial awareness that empowers them to make wise choices.

Start by creating a shopping list at home, a tool that keeps your household organized and is a practical way to teach your child about needs and wants. Sit down with them and discuss what the family requires for the week. Items like bread, milk, and fruit fall into the "needs" category—essentials for daily life. Then, talk about the "wants"—those extra treats or snacks that are nice but unnecessary. By categorizing items this way, you help your child understand the difference and prioritize accordingly. This exercise encourages them to think critically about spending and recognize that while wanting to bring temporary joy, it needs to fulfill essential purposes.

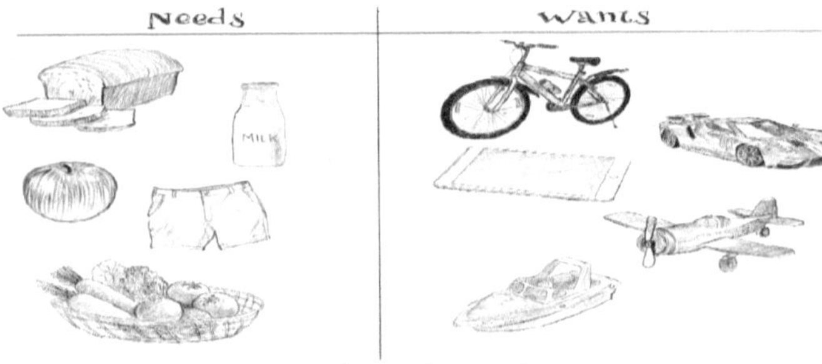

Needs and Wants

Next, introduce intelligent shopping strategies that can make every trip an exercise in financial literacy. Show your child how to compare prices by examining different brands and sizes of an item. Explain how sometimes the more extensive package isn't always the better deal and how sales can offer savings if approached wisely. You can even turn it into a game: Challenge them to find the best price for a product on the list. This makes shopping more engaging and teaches them valuable skills like price comparison and critical evaluation. Scanning the shelves teaches them to be discerning consumers, making choices based on value rather than impulse.

To make this lesson even more impactful:

1. Engage your child in a role-playing activity that simulates a shopping experience.
2. Set up a mock store at home using items from your pantry or toy collection.
3. Give your child a set amount of play money and let them "shop" for what they need.
4. As they make their selections, encourage them to consider whether each item is a need or a want and how their choices affect their budget.

Mom and Son discussing what items to get from the pantry

This interactive approach helps solidify the concepts in a fun and memorable way. It allows them to experiment with decision-making in a safe environment, building confidence and understanding that can be applied in real-life scenarios.

Discuss the impact of impulse buying, a common challenge that can derail even the best-laid financial plans. Kids, like adults, can be tempted by the immediate gratification of an unplanned purchase. Use relatable examples to highlight how buying a candy bar on a whim can affect their ability to save for a larger goal. This conversation can lead to a deeper understanding of how unchecked spending can chip away at savings, leaving less for essential purchases. By helping your child recognize the signs of impulse buying, you equip them with the self-awareness to pause and consider their choices before purchasing.

Reflection Section: Spotting Impulse Buys

Here's a simple exercise to try during your next shopping trip: As you walk the aisles, encourage your child to identify items that catch their eye as impulse buys. Discuss why those items appeal to them and how they can decide whether they're worth purchasing. This reflection helps them become more mindful consumers, aware of the emotional and external factors influencing their spending. By practicing this skill regularly, they develop a keen sense of financial discipline that supports their ability to make thoughtful, deliberate choices.

Through these engaging activities and discussions, you can transform routine shopping trips into valuable lessons in financial literacy. By teaching your child to differentiate between needs and wants, employ intelligent shopping strategies, and recognize the impact of impulse buying, you empower them to make informed decisions. As they grow, these skills will become second nature, guiding them as they navigate the complex world of personal finance with confidence and clarity.

THE ADVENTURE OF SPENDING WISELY

Imagine a child named Jack who loves adventures and is always up for a challenge. One day, Jack's parents gave him a small sum of money to spend however he liked, and Jack felt like he was holding a treasure chest. He immediately thought about all the toys and gadgets he could buy. But his parents suggested he think carefully and plan how to use it. This was new territory for Jack, who usually spent his money as soon as he got it. He decided to embark on a quest that would teach him how to spend wisely and see the consequences of his choices. Jack's journey began with a simple map his parents helped him draw. It showed two paths: one leading to a fun, immediate purchase and the other to something he needed, like a new pair of shoes for school. Jack loved his old ones, but they were getting too tight. On one hand, he could spend his money on the latest action figure his friends were buzzing about. On the other, he could invest in something that would keep his feet comfy and ready for all his playground adventures. Jack spent a day weighing his options, imagining the thrill of showing off the toy and the relief of wearing shoes that didn't pinch.

Jack ponders ... "Should I take the Wants path or the Needs path?"

Amid his decision-making, Jack's parents introduced him to a simple concept: planning before purchasing. They explained that a bit of thought before spending could lead to more satisfaction in the long run. Jack learned to list the pros and cons of each choice. Sure, the toy was exciting, but the shoes were a necessity that would benefit him daily. They also taught him about saving part of his money for future goals, something Jack hadn't considered before. He realized he could eventually afford the shoes and the toy by saving even a tiny portion. This revelation was like unlocking a new level in his quest, opening doors to possibilities he hadn't seen. Jack also realized that making a wise choice didn't mean giving up on fun. It was about balancing—enjoying the present while planning for the future.

As Jack pondered, his parents shared a story from their childhood, when they had to choose between instant gratification and long-term gain. They spoke of lessons learned and how those choices shaped their understanding of money. Inspired, Jack decided to take a practical approach. He would buy the shoes, ensuring comfort for his daily escapades, and save a bit for the toy. He felt proud of his decision, knowing it was well thought out and beneficial in more ways than one. This choice taught him about prioritizing needs and setting realistic goals. Jack's parents praised his decision, reinforcing his newfound confidence in handling money. They reminded him that spending wisely leads to fulfilling needs and objectives more effectively, a lesson Jack could carry forward.

In the end, Jack's adventure in spending wisely was more than just a single decision; it was a series of thought processes, reflections, and realizations that transformed his perspective on money. The moral was clear: Wise spending isn't about denying fun but making choices that align with your goals and values. Jack learned that with careful planning and patience, he could enjoy the essentials and the extras, setting the stage for future financial adventures. This experience empowered him to take charge of his spending habits, turning every purchase into an opportunity to learn and grow. Jack's story reminds us that the path to financial wisdom is paved with curiosity, reflection, and the courage to make choices that honor our needs and dreams.

BUDGETING BASICS: CREATING A SIMPLE BUDGET

Imagine this: Your child just received their weekly allowance, and they are excited, dreaming about everything they might buy. But before that money burns a hole in their pocket, it's the perfect time to introduce them to the concept of a budget. Think of a budget as a financial roadmap—a plan outlining where money comes from and where it goes. It helps us understand our income and expenses, ensuring we don't spend more than we have. For kids, a budget can be a simple chart or a colorful sheet that breaks down their allowance into different categories. This teaches them how to manage money and empowers them to make informed choices, setting the stage for intelligent financial habits.

Creating a budget is like assembling a puzzle, where each piece represents a part of the financial picture. Start by helping your child list their income sources. This might include their weekly allowance, birthday money, or earnings from small chores. Once they understand how much money they have, guide them in estimating their expenses. These could include saving for a new toy, buying art supplies, or setting aside money for a family outing. By categorizing expenses, children learn to prioritize and allocate their funds wisely. This exercise helps them see the bigger picture, making it easier to decide where to spend, save, or give. Please encourage them to set aside a portion for savings, reinforcing the lesson that saving is essential to financial planning.

Saving & Expenses Tracker

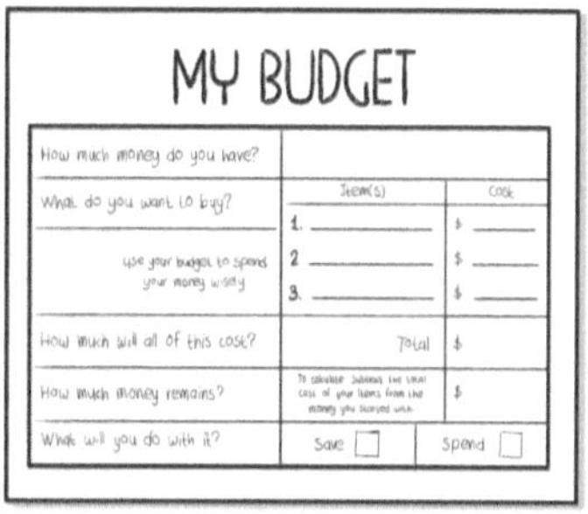

Budget Template Idea

To make budgeting engaging, consider using interactive activities that involve creating their own budgets. Provide templates where they can fill in their income and expenses, adding a splash of color with markers or stickers. This hands-on approach makes budgeting tangible and fun, transforming what might seem tedious into an enjoyable learning experience. As they work through the activity, discuss the importance of balancing their budget and the benefits of having a plan. By visualizing their budget, children gain a clearer understanding of their financial situation, making it easier to stick to their plans and reach their goals. This interaction solidifies their budgeting grasp and builds confidence in their ability to manage money.

Life is unpredictable, and sometimes expenses pop up unexpectedly. Teaching your child how to adjust their budget in response to changes is a valuable skill. Present a scenario where they face an unexpected expense, like a school field trip or a birthday gift for a friend. Discuss how they might need to re-evaluate their budget, shifting money from one category to another to accommodate this new priority. This exercise shows them the flexibility required in financial planning and the importance of being prepared for surprises. They develop resilience and problem-solving skills as they learn to adapt their budget, preparing them for real-world financial challenges. Please encourage them to think creatively about solutions, perhaps finding ways to earn a little extra or deciding to forgo a more minor expense to cover the new cost.

Budgeting is more than just numbers on a page; it's a tool that empowers children to take control of their finances. Engaging them in the process instills a sense of responsibility and independence. They understand that money management involves making choices that align with their goals and values. As they practice budgeting, they gain insights into their spending habits and learn to prioritize what truly matters. This skill becomes a cornerstone of their financial literacy, guiding them as they grow and face more complex financial decisions. Through budgeting, children learn the mechanics of managing money and build a foundation for a lifetime of thoughtful financial planning.

THE STORY OF LUCY'S LEMONADE STAND

It all started on a warm summer day when Lucy stared out her window, watching the neighborhood kids enjoying their icy treats. Inspiration struck her like a lightning bolt. She set up her very own lemonade stand right in her front yard. Lucy's eyes twinkled with excitement as she imagined the line of thirsty customers. Her mom was on board with the idea, so together, they made a list of what they needed: lemons, sugar, cups, and a sturdy table. To attract attention, Lucy even made a bright sign that read "Lucy's Lemonade: Fresh and Sweet!" With her setup complete, she felt like a true entrepreneur, ready to take on the world one cup at a time.

Running the lemonade stand turned out to be more than just pouring drinks. Lucy quickly realized she had to manage her earnings wisely. As the coins jingled into her cash box, she thought about everything she could buy. But her mom gently reminded her that the money she spent on supplies had to come out first. This meant Lucy needed to calculate her costs before counting her profits. They sat together, tallying up the expenses. Lucy learned that spending less on supplies would shrink her earnings, leaving less for her piggy bank. This was her first real lesson in financial management.

Lucy faced a big decision: How much should she charge for each cup? She wanted to be fair but make enough to cover her costs and earn a little extra. After some thought, they settled on a price that seemed just right, balancing affordability with profitability. The day flew by as Lucy served cup after cup, smiling at each satisfied customer. Lucy was ready to count her earnings when the sun dipped below the horizon. Her mom helped her with the math, subtracting the cost of supplies from her total sales. The profit she saw was more than just numbers; it was the fruit of her hard work and intelligent decisions.

Lucy's Lemonade Stand

Lucy also discovered the value of reinvesting her profits to grow her business. Instead of spending all her earnings on toys, she saved part to buy more supplies for another lemonade stand day. This way, she could keep her business going and earn even more. Lucy realized that reinvestment was like planting seeds for future growth. She ensured she could continue her venture by setting aside some of her profits and learning more with each experience. Her lemonade stand taught her about planning, foresight, and the benefits of thinking long term.

As Lucy pondered her success, she felt a sense of pride and joy. She understood the value of innovative financial management and how it could help her achieve her goals. Her lemonade stand was more than just a summer activity; it was a stepping stone to understanding the world of business and finance. Lucy learned that she could turn a simple idea into something rewarding with a little effort and wise choices. Her story is a testament to the power of initiative, creativity, and financial savvy. Lucy's adventure with her lemonade stand began her journey of learning and growing, one cup at a time.

LEARNING FROM MISTAKES: SPENDING TOO MUCH

There comes a time when every child experiences the thrill of receiving money, only to find it vanishing faster than anticipated. It's an all-too-common scenario: Your child eagerly spends their entire allowance on a shiny new toy, only to realize they no longer have enough left for the outing they had planned with friends. This lesson in overspending can be a decisive teaching moment, highlighting the consequences of exceeding budget limits. When children spend more than they have, they might miss out on their goals, like saving for a coveted item or contributing to a special event. This understanding is crucial, laying the foundation for more responsible financial behavior. By discussing these outcomes openly, you can help your child connect their spending habits with the impact on their plans, encouraging them to think twice before making impulsive purchases.

The good news is that overspending is not the end of the world. In fact, it presents a perfect opportunity to introduce problem-solving strategies that can correct these habits. Start by helping your child set spending limits. Together, you can establish clear guidelines for how much they can spend on wants versus how much they should save for needs. Please encourage them to track their expenses, perhaps in a small notebook or with the help of an app designed for kids. This simple practice allows them to see where their money goes and identify patterns in their spending. Over time, they can develop a keen sense of financial awareness, learning to adjust their habits based on their goals and priorities. By setting boundaries and monitoring their expenses, children gain the tools to manage their money more effectively, reducing the likelihood of overspending in the future.

Reflective activities can further deepen your child's understanding of their spending decisions. Please encourage them to journal about a time when they overspent and what led to that choice. What was the item, and why did it seem so important now? How did they feel afterward, and what did they learn from the experience? This reflection can be enlightening, helping them pinpoint the motivations behind their spending and recognize any emotions that influenced their decisions. Children can gain clarity and perspective by writing down their thoughts and turning past mistakes into valuable lessons. This process fosters self-awareness and empowers them to make more informed choices in the future as they learn to align their spending with their values and goals.

Mistakes, as it turns out, are not something to be feared but embraced. They provide rich opportunities for growth and learning, especially when managing money. Emphasize to your child that making mistakes is a natural part of life and essential to gaining wisdom. When they acknowledge and reflect on their missteps, they can develop better financial habits moving forward. Each mistake becomes a stepping stone toward greater financial literacy, equipping them with the insights to navigate more complex financial landscapes as they grow. By fostering an environment where mistakes are seen as opportunities rather than failures, you can encourage your child to approach their finances with curiosity and confidence, ready to learn and adapt to each new experience.

NEEDS, WANTS, AND THE ART OF NEGOTIATION

Negotiation is a skill that can serve children well throughout their lives, and it's never too early to start learning. Think of negotiation as a friendly discussion aimed at reaching an agreement.. It's about finding a middle ground where both parties feel satisfied. Negotiation can be a valuable tool when it comes to allowances or chores. For instance, your child might want a bit more allowance for completing extra chores. This opens the door for a conversation where they can present their case, and you can share your expectations. Through this process, they learn to communicate their needs clearly and understand the importance of compromise. It's not about winning or losing but reaching an agreement that works for everyone involved. Negotiation teaches kids to express themselves effectively while considering the perspective of others, fostering empathy and understanding.

Role-playing is a fantastic way to practice these skills in a low-pressure setting. Set up scenarios where your child can negotiate for something they desire, like a toy or extra screen time. You can take turns playing different roles, such as the parent or the shopkeeper, to give them a broader view of negotiation dynamics. This activity allows them to practice crafting arguments, listening actively, and finding mutually beneficial solutions. It's a safe space to make mistakes and learn from them, building confidence in their ability to navigate real-life negotiations. Through role-playing, children discover that negotiation is a respectful dialogue where both sides can express their views and work toward a common goal. These mock negotiations help them understand the give-and-take nature of discussions, preparing them for more complex situations in the future.

Negotiation can also help children find the balance between their needs and wants. For example, if your child wants to buy a toy but needs new school supplies, you can guide them to negotiate a compromise. They may agree to save part of their allowance for the toy while allocating funds for their school needs. This teaches them to prioritize and make thoughtful decisions that satisfy both their immediate desires and their essential needs. It's a lesson in understanding that life often requires balancing different priorities, and negotiation can help achieve that balance. By practicing negotiation, children learn to weigh their options and find solutions that address their wants and needs. This skill is invaluable as they grow and face more complex financial decisions, helping them navigate the challenges of budgeting and spending wisely.

Engaging in interactive negotiation games can further enhance these skills. You might set up a game where children negotiate trades or deal with their peers, simulating real-world scenarios in a playful context. These games encourage creativity and teamwork as kids brainstorm ways to achieve their objectives while considering the needs of others. Through these interactions, they learn to be persuasive yet fair, honing their ability to articulate their thoughts and ideas. Such games can be both educational and enjoyable, reinforcing the lessons of negotiation in a fun and engaging manner. By turning negotiation into a game, children are more likely to embrace and apply the concept in their daily lives. They see negotiation not as a chore but as an opportunity to collaborate and achieve shared goals, fostering a positive approach to problem-solving and communication.

The Great Lemonade Stand Negotiation

Children also learn valuable financial practices and concepts through the art of storytelling. Here's a delightful story about negotiation that you can share with your child:

Once upon a time, in the cheerful town of Sunnyville, there was an ambitious 11-year-old named Alex. Alex had a brilliant idea: to set up a lemonade stand on a hot summer day to earn some extra allowance. Excited about the prospect of running their own little business, Alex ran to the kitchen to gather supplies.

On the day of the stand, Alex spent hours squeezing lemons, mixing sugar, and pouring the refreshing lemonade into cups. But there was one problem: Alex needed help! So, Alex called his best friend, Sam, to join the fun.

After a quick brainstorming session, they decided that splitting the work and profits would be the best option. However, when Sam arrived, they realized they had different ideas about how to run things. Alex wanted to sell the lemonade for $1 a cup, while Sam thought they should price it at $1.50 since it was so refreshing.

Feeling that they needed to split the profits based on their contributions, Alex proposed their idea to Sam. "How about we agree that if we sell each cup for $1, we can sell more and attract more customers? That way, we can each take home some good money at the end of the day!"

Sam paused and thought about it. "But if we charge $1.50, we'd make more money on each cup! We could still sell at least a few at that price. Let's work out a deal!"

That's when Alex remembered what their parents taught them about negotiation. So Alex suggested, "How about we start at $1.50 for the first half of the day? We can lower sales to $1 after lunch if sales are slow. This way, we can see which one works better!"

Sam's eyes lit up. "That sounds fair! We could also try to attract customers with a sign that mentions a special deal! If they buy two cups, we'll charge them $2.50 instead of $3."

Both friends grinned, realizing they were on a roll. They talked about what their signs would say and how they could get more people to come, deciding on fun decorations like colorful balloons. Sam ran to the nearby craft store while Alex set up the stand.

As the day went on, their lemonade stand became the talk of Sunnyville! They shouted, "Cold lemonade! Only $1.50 or two for $2.50!" They sold out quickly. They even decided to reduce the price to $1 during their busy hours after noticing some customers hesitating, just as they'd planned.

At the end of the day, they counted the money. They were surprised by how much they earned together: even more than they had anticipated! Alex and Sam realized that by negotiating their ideas and finding a compromise, they created a fantastic lemonade stand that made a profit and was so much fun!

Alex and Sam negotiating

Alex smiled as they walked home with their earnings and said, "Negotiation really works! It's not just about one person winning; it's about coming together and sharing ideas to make something good for us."

Sam nodded, "Definitely! I can't wait to try this out again next summer. Who knows what we can come up with next time?"

From that day forward, Alex and Sam carried the lessons of negotiation with them, ready for any adventure that came their way!

In learning the art of negotiation, children gain more than just the ability to discuss allowances or chores. They develop essential life skills, including effective communication, critical thinking, and empathy. These skills empower them to express their needs while respecting the viewpoints of others, leading to more harmonious interactions at home, in school, and beyond. As they practice negotiating, they become more confident handling various situations, from deciding what to spend their money on to resolving conflicts with peers. Through negotiation, children learn that collaboration and compromise can lead to solutions that benefit everyone, setting the stage for successful relationships and decision-making in the future.

4

INTRODUCTION TO INVESTING

Picture this: A sunny afternoon in the garden, where your child is busy planting seeds in the soil, eagerly anticipating the growth of vibrant plants. This simple act of gardening mirrors the fundamental concept of investing. Just as seeds need time, care, and the right conditions to flourish into beautiful flowers, investing involves putting your money into something with the expectation of seeing it grow over time. Imagine explaining to your child that investing is like planting a financial seed—a little bit of money today can become more tomorrow if tended to wisely. This chapter introduces the exciting investing world through relatable analogies and practical examples, demystifying what might initially seem complex and making it accessible to young learners.

Investing is all about the potential for growth. It's putting your money into a particular venture or asset, hoping it will increase in value over time. Think of it as nurturing a young plant. It can grow into a sturdy tree with enough sunlight and water. Similarly, by investing money wisely, it can grow and provide benefits down the road. Whether it's saving for college or a future car, investing has the potential to yield substantial returns, emphasizing the importance of long-term planning. Investing involves more strategy and patience than simply saving money in a jar. Still, the rewards can be much more significant. It's like watching that little seed sprout and eventually bear fruit, providing sustenance and shade for years.

Engaging children in interactive activities can further solidify these concepts. Imagine setting up a pretend lemonade stand investment scenario at home. Give your child a small amount of pretend money and let them decide whether to buy stock in the lemonade stand (a share of the profits) or lend money as a bond (collecting interest over time). Track their investment's growth over a few weeks, adjusting based on the pretend stand's "performance." This hands-on activity makes investing tangible and encourages critical thinking and decision-making. It's an adventure where they can see their financial seed grow, learning valuable lessons about investing in a fun and engaging way.

Interactive Activity: Investment Growth Chart

Create an interactive growth chart to visualize potential investment returns over time. Use a piece of poster board divided into months or years. Let your child place stickers or draw symbols representing their investments as they metaphorically grow. This visual representation helps them see the progression of investments, making the abstract idea of financial growth more concrete and exciting. By monitoring this chart, children can grasp the concept of compound growth, reinforcing the benefits of investing early and consistently. This activity nurtures a sense of curiosity and excitement about finance, encouraging them to explore the world of investing further.

This chapter aims to make investing accessible and exciting for young learners through relatable analogies and engaging activities. By introducing essential concepts such as stocks, bonds, and the purpose of investing, children can develop a foundational understanding of how money can work for them over time. Investing is not just about numbers; it's about planting seeds for the future, watching them grow, and enjoying the fruits of careful planning and patience.

THE MAGIC TREE: UNDERSTANDING GROWTH

Imagine a magical tree in your backyard, one that starts as a tiny sapling but, with time and care, grows into a magnificent, towering tree laden with fruit. This tree doesn't just sprout overnight; it needs water, sunlight, and patience. Investing works much the same way. It's not about instant results but nurturing and watching your financial seeds grow over time. Just like that tree, investments need the right conditions to flourish. By explaining this to your child, you can show them that, with a bit of patience and care, their investments can grow strong and bear fruit. The fruits of this tree represent the returns on their investments, the rewards for their patience and intelligent decisions.

Growth over time is a crucial part of investing. Explain to your child that investments need time to mature, just as a tree takes years to grow. The longer you allow your investments to grow, the bigger they can become. It's like watching a tree that you planted as a seedling gradually stretch its branches toward the sky, year after year. Each year, the tree becomes sturdier and produces more fruit, reflecting how investments can increase in value over time. The key here is time; the earlier you start investing, the more time your investments have to grow. This concept helps children understand the importance of starting early and being patient. Children can see how steady, consistent nurturing leads to significant growth by drawing parallels between a growing tree and their savings.

To help visualize this concept, consider a creative exercise where your child can create a growth timeline for their investments. They could draw a series of trees on a timeline, each representing different stages of growth. In the beginning, the tree is small with few leaves, but as time progresses, it gains more branches and eventually bears fruit. Please encourage them to mark important milestones along the timeline, such as reaching a particular savings goal or learning a new investing strategy. This visual representation not only makes the concept of investment growth tangible but also allows them to track their progress and celebrate achievements along the way. This exercise turns abstract financial growth into something they can see and understand, reinforcing the lessons of patience and discipline.

Patience plays a pivotal role in both growing a tree and nurturing investments. Just as a tree doesn't bear fruit immediately, investments require time to yield returns. It might be tempting for your child to want quick results, but teaching them the value of patience can lead to more substantial rewards. It's about helping them understand that the wait is worthwhile, as the fruits of their patience can be enjoyed for years. This lesson in patience isn't just about money; it's about developing the ability to wait for a reward, a valuable life skill that applies to many aspects of life. By waiting for the tree to bear fruit, your child learns that good things come to those who patiently nurture their investments with care.

Luna and the Magical Investment Garden

Once upon a time, in the sunny village of Greenfield, there lived an 11-year-old girl named Luna. Luna was curious and loved nature, especially the big, beautiful trees surrounding her home. Her wise grandfather visited one bright day, bringing a mysterious box filled with seeds.

"Luna," he said with a twinkle in his eye, "these aren't just any seeds; they're magical investment seeds! If you care for them, they will grow into a magnificent tree with special fruits—fruits of your investments!"

Intrigued, Luna asked, "What do I need to do to help the seeds grow?"

Her grandfather smiled and explained, "Like trees need water and sunlight, these seeds need patience, care, and some regular contributions. If you want this tree to flourish, you must treat it well over time."

Excited to start her journey, Luna planted the seeds in her backyard garden. Every day after school, she watered them, ensured they got enough sunlight, and even talked to them as if they could hear her. Luna imagined her tree stretching high into the sky, laden with golden fruits that represented the future rewards of her hard work and patience.

As the weeks passed, Luna sometimes felt disappointed. The seeds began to sprout tiny green leaves, but very slowly. "Why isn't my tree growing faster?" she wondered. Just then, her grandfather visited again and noticed her concern.

"Remember, Luna," he said gently, "great things take time. You planted a tiny seed today, but it'll become a strong tree if you keep caring for it. When you study or practice something, the results come with consistent effort!"

Inspired, Luna decided to set some goals for her garden. She made a colorful chart on a big piece of paper. At the top was a picture of a small sapling, and at the bottom was an image of a tall, fruitful tree. She marked her progress each month: the leaves grew more extensive, and the trunk became sturdier.

"What if I plant more seeds?" Luna thought. "Could that make me grow my investment quicker?" So, she decided to save part of her weekly allowance to buy more seeds. With her savings and hard work, she planted five more magical seeds next to the first.

As time passed, she could finally see the growth she had hoped for! The once-tiny saplings had now turned into tall trees adorned with bright, shining fruits, the different colors representing different investments. Luna felt a sense of pride, knowing that her dedication was paying off.

One day, Luna's friends came over to admire her garden. They were amazed by the colorful fruit hanging from the branches. "Wow, what's the secret?" they asked.

Luna excitedly shared, "It's all about patience and nurturing! These fruits represent the rewards of my investments. The more I took care of them, the more they grew!"

As the summer drew close, Luna decided it was time to harvest some of the magical fruit. When she and her friends took a bite, they found that each fruit had a unique flavor: some were tangy, others sweet, but they all brought a smile to their faces.

That day, Luna shared the fruits and her story of growth—the joy of planting today for the rewards of tomorrow. She encouraged her friends to grow their own seeds in the garden and their savings.

As they finished their delicious feast, Luna realized that investing was like nurturing her magical garden: it required time, effort, and patience. And the fruits they enjoyed were just the beginning of a lifelong journey of growth.

Luna nurturing her magical investment seeds patiently giving then time to grow and bear fruit.

From then on, Luna and her friends eagerly tended their gardens. They watched their magical trees blossom, learning together that great things come to those who nurture their seeds today!

The metaphor of the magic seeds serves as a beautiful illustration of how investments grow over time. It captures the essence of investing—nurturing your financial seeds, giving them time to mature, and reaping the rewards of patience and intelligent decision-making. Through this story, children can learn that investing is a process, not a sprint. It's about planting seeds today that can provide for tomorrow, teaching them to appreciate the journey of growth and the joy of seeing their efforts come to fruition. This understanding lays a foundation for lifelong financial habits, encouraging them to think long term and make thoughtful decisions that align with their goals and values.

RISK AND REWARD: BALANCING YOUR CHOICES

Imagine your child learning to ride a bike for the first time. There's a chance they might fall, but there's also the thrill of eventually pedaling down the street with the wind in their hair. This is much like the concept of risk in investing. Investing comes with risks because there's the possibility of losing money. As falling off a bike is risky, putting money into an investment might not always go as planned. But without taking that risk, the reward—like the joy of riding a bike confidently—might never be realized. Teaching kids about risk helps them understand that not all investments are guaranteed to grow. Still, carefully considering the potential rewards can be well worth it.

On the flip side, the reward aspect of investing makes it exciting. Higher risks can lead to higher rewards, a lesson that can be taught through everyday experiences. Think about trying a new strategy in a game. The risk is uncertain, but the victory feels even sweeter if it pays off. For example, suppose your child decides to try a new move in a board game. In that case, they might initially feel unsure, but winning the game because of that move shows them the potential rewards of taking calculated risks. This teaches children that while risk is part of the process, the possibility of reward makes it worthwhile. It's about finding that balance—understanding that some risks are worth taking but must be weighed carefully.

Consider engaging with your child through scenarios where they must weigh risks and rewards. One day, they might invest their savings into a pretend business, like a toy company. They could visualize the excitement of seeing their investment grow if the business succeeds but also recognize the possibility of losing some of their money if it doesn't. Through such scenarios, children can practice making decisions by evaluating both sides of the equation. This exercise allows them to explore the concept of risk versus reward in a safe and controlled environment, preparing them for similar choices they may face in the future. It's a valuable lesson in decision-making, teaching them to assess situations and make informed choices that align with their goals.

It's an essential part of managing risk. It's as research. Encourage children to gather information before making investment decisions, just as they would before trying out a new hobby or activity. This involves learning about the market or the product they're interested in. For instance, if they're considering investing in that pretend toy business, they could research what makes certain toys popular or what kids are currently interested in. Doing this minimizes risks and increases their chances of making successful investments. Teaching children to value research instills a sense of curiosity and diligence, helping them become more informed investors. It's about equipping them with the skills to analyze and understand the world around them, leading to better financial decisions.

Incorporating these lessons into everyday conversations can make them more relatable and memorable for your child. Discussing risks and rewards in contexts they understand helps demystify the complexities of investing. It's not just about money; it's about making choices that balance potential gains and possible losses. By involving them in these discussions, you empower them to think critically and develop a healthy approach to risk-taking. This understanding will serve them well in financial matters and life as they learn to navigate challenges and opportunities confidently.

THE TALE OF THE YOUNG INVESTOR

Once upon a time, a curious young boy named Alex lived in a bustling city surrounded by tall buildings and the hum of everyday life. Alex was not just any child; he had an insatiable curiosity about how the world worked, especially regarding money. One day, after a particularly engaging lesson at school about the wonders of saving, Alex decided he wanted to learn more about investing. His parents, supportive and excited about his newfound interest, gave him a small amount of money. They explained that investing was a way to make money grow, just like planting a tiny seed and watching it turn into a flourishing plant.

Armed with his initial investment, Alex set out to learn everything he could. He began by exploring different types of investments, starting with stocks. Alex understood that buying a stock meant owning a little piece of a company. At first, he was drawn to investing in companies that made fun and exciting products, like video games and toys. But his dad suggested he think about diversifying his investments. This meant not putting all his money into one type of stock but spreading it across different industries to manage risk. Alex found this idea fascinating, realizing that diversification could make his investment portfolio healthier and more robust, just like not eating the same daily lunch.

With this new knowledge, Alex faced his first big decision: Should he invest in a tech company buzzing with innovation or a traditional company known for its steady growth? He pondered his options, thinking about the excitement and potential of the tech sector and the stability offered by the conventional company. In the end, Alex chose a bit of both, deciding that a mix would give him the thrill of potentially high returns while also providing a safety net with the traditional stock. This choice taught him to balance his investments and make thoughtful decisions based on research and personal goals.

As time passed, Alex diligently tracked his investments, learning from each experience. He observed how some stocks soared while others dipped, teaching him the natural ebb and flow of the market. Through it all, Alex discovered that investing wasn't just about numbers; it was about understanding the world and making informed choices. He learned to keep a cool head during market fluctuations, knowing that ups and downs were part of the investing landscape. This lesson was invaluable, teaching him patience and resilience. Alex enjoyed seeing his small investment portfolio grow and firsthand the rewards of his calculated decisions.

Through his adventures in investing, Alex realized that knowledge and experience were his most excellent tools. Each decision, whether a triumph or a setback, added to his understanding of finance. He became more confident, not just in managing his money but in knowing that he could navigate the complexities of the financial world. For Alex, investing was no longer a mysterious concept but a journey filled with learning and growth. He discovered that, with the right mindset, investing could lead to financial independence and the freedom to pursue his dreams. Alex's story inspires us all to embrace learning, take calculated risks, and trust in the power of thoughtful investing.

Alex observing the natural ebb and flow of the stock market

STOCKS, BONDS, AND OTHER FUN STUFF

Imagine your child sitting at the kitchen table, a slice of their favorite pie in front of them. Now, ask them to picture that pie as a company, and each slice represents a share of that company. When someone buys a stock, they purchase a slice of that company pie. If the company does well, the value of each slice increases, offering a tasty reward for those who own it. Stocks can be an exciting way for your child to understand ownership and value growth. They can visualize how being a part of a company's success means their slice of the pie might get bigger, offering more tasty benefits over time.

Now, picture your child lending a toy to a friend with the promise that the friend will return it after a week and give him a little extra as a thank-you. This is a lot like what bonds are. Bonds are like little IOUs. When your child invests in a bond, they lend money to a company or government. In return, they receive interest, similar to the extra thank-you from their friend. Bonds can be fascinating for kids because they involve trust and return. You can even use Legos to build a "company" and have your child "lend" Monopoly money to it, receiving interest paid monthly or quarterly. This playful approach brings the abstract idea of bonds to life, making it easier for kids to understand how loans can generate income over time.

ABC Company one slice represents 1 stock or 1 share

Sample explanation of what a Bond is

Beyond stocks and bonds, other investment options exist, like mutual funds and real estate. Mutual funds are a bit like a basket of stocks. Instead of buying individual stocks, kids can think of mutual funds as owning a whole basket filled with different types of fruits—apples, oranges, and bananas. If one fruit doesn't do well, the others might still thrive, balancing the overall value. On the other hand, real estate involves owning property like houses or land. It's like having a piece of land where they can build their Lego city. These options broaden the investing horizon, showing children multiple paths to growing wealth, each with flavor and potential.

Example of a mutual fund where each fruit represent a different kind of compnay

Consider setting up a pretend investment:

1. Consider engaging your child in these concepts.
2. Gather some play money and a variety of pretend investment options—maybe some Lego blocks for real estate, Monopoly money for bonds, and cut-out pictures of companies for stocks.
3. Get your child to decide how to distribute their resources, simulating the choice between different types of investments.

They can track their portfolio over time, adjusting as they see fit. This interactive exploration not only makes investing fun but also encourages strategic thinking. Your child learns to balance risk and reward, understanding how diversifying their investments can lead to more stable growth.

Introducing these concepts through relatable examples and interactive activities gives your child a foundational understanding of investing. They begin to see the potential of their financial seeds and how they can sprout and flourish in various ways. Stocks, bonds, mutual funds, and real estate offer unique opportunities, and exploring these options can ignite a curiosity that inspires them to learn more about finance. With this knowledge, they gain the confidence to make informed decisions, discovering the joy of watching their investments grow and the fulfillment of achieving their financial goals.

THE STORY OF SAMMY'S STOCK MARKET ADVENTURE

Meet Sammy, a curious and adventurous child with a knack for building intricate LEGO cities and dreaming big. One day, while visiting his uncle, who worked in the bustling heart of downtown, Sammy's attention was captured by a large screen displaying the stock market's dizzying dance of numbers and arrows. Curious, Sammy asked, "Uncle, what are all those numbers?" His uncle explained that they represented the stock market. In this place, people buy and sell parts of companies, hoping their value will increase. Intrigued, Sammy decided he wanted to learn more about this fascinating world.

Eager to dive in, Sammy's uncle offered him a small sum to start his first stock purchase. Sammy chose to invest in a company that made his favorite video games. With some guidance, he learned to read stock charts like maps showing whether a company's stock was climbing the mountain of success or sliding down a slope. At first, it was just a jumble of lines, but soon, Sammy began to see patterns. He noticed how the lines would go up when a new game was launched or drop if the reviews weren't stellar. This new skill was like cracking a code, and Sammy felt a thrill each time he deciphered the charts' secrets.

As Sammy's adventure continued, he found himself at a crossroads. One day, the stock of his chosen company took a sharp dip. His uncle explained that this was a common occurrence, much like the weather, which can change suddenly. Sammy had to decide whether to hold on to or sell his stock before it fell further. He remembered his uncle's advice about making informed decisions and not rushing based on fear. Sammy had trusted that the company's upcoming game release could turn the tide. It was a test of patience and belief, which he realized were crucial in the stock market.

This interactive journey taught Sammy the importance of market trends and price changes. He discovered that as seasons affect the weather, different factors influence stock prices, from company performance to global events. Sammy's uncle encouraged him to research and stay informed, making him a young detective, piecing together clues from news articles and company reports. In this process of investigation and understanding, Sammy found a deeper appreciation for the world of investing. He saw firsthand how knowledge and timing could transform a small investment into something more.

Sammy thinking about whether he should hold or sell since stock is falling sharply.

With each decision, Sammy gained valuable insights. He realized that investing wasn't just about luck or guessing. It was about understanding the market, making educated choices, and learning from successes and setbacks. Sammy's journey taught him the power of research and patience—how gathering information and waiting for the right moment could lead to better outcomes. This adventure in the stock market wasn't just about numbers but about growing wiser and more confident. Sammy's story reminds us all that anyone can navigate the complex world of investing with curiosity, a willingness to learn, and a bit of courage.

As we wrap up Sammy's adventure, we've explored how investing can be a fun and educational experience. Sammy's story shows us that understanding the market and making informed decisions are keys to success. Now that we've equipped you with the basics of investing, it's time to dive into the next chapter, where we explore financial responsibility and how these early lessons can set the stage for intelligent money management in the future.

HELP BUILD A FINANCIALLY SAVVY GENERATION

> *"Sometimes parents wait until their kids are in their teens before they start talking about managing money — when they could be starting when their kids are in preschool."*
>
> — WARREN BUFFETT

I'd love it if you could take a pause in your reading journey to think about Warren Buffett's belief in the importance of instilling a money mindset in kids practically from a very early age. One study by Cambridge University academics found that children between the ages of three and four are able to grasp basic money concepts. By seven, they have already developed basic concepts that impact their future financial behaviors. The sooner you help your child understand that they are in control of money rather than vice versa, the greater the likelihood they will build a healthy relationship with money. Once your child knows the importance of concepts like budgeting, saving, and growing their money through investment, they will be less likely to get into bad debt and have money worries.

By sharing the ideas, information, and strategies in this book for everything from wise spending to building passive wealth through investment, you are empowering your child to view money through a positive lens. When your child knows the value of earning, saving, and investing money, they can do things later in life like invest in a good education, travel the world, and do their part to give back to the community. You are, in a way, giving them the gift of a smart relationship with money… one in which they feel confident, empowered, and secure. If you find that the ideas and activities I've suggested so far are offering you a dynamic, structured, efficient way to share the keys to financial empowerment with your child, please take just one minute to share your opinion.

By leaving a review of this book on Amazon, you'll help another parent share smart money strategies with their children.

It will only take a minute, but it could spark a chain reaction that helps children across the globe understand that achieving success with money is *their* decision.

Scan the QR code below

5

FINANCIAL RESPONSIBILITY

Imagine a bustling kitchen on a Saturday morning, where the smell of pancakes fills the air and laughter echoes as your child counts out their weekly allowance. This moment is ripe with potential for teaching financial responsibility. Making wise choices with money is a skill that will serve them well throughout life. It's about more than just saving or spending; it's about understanding the impact of their decisions on their future. As parents, you can guide them toward making thoughtful financial choices, empowering them to take control of their financial health from a young age.

MAKING RESPONSIBLE CHOICES: EVERYDAY DECISIONS

The first step in teaching children responsible financial choices is introducing them to decision-making skills. This involves showing them how to evaluate their options and make choices that align with their goals. One way to start is by discussing saving part of their allowance instead of spending it all at once. Please encourage them to think about what they genuinely want and can wait for. This practice teaches them patience and the satisfaction that comes from achieving a goal through careful planning and saving.

Everyday financial choices can have long-term effects on their economic well-being. For instance, deciding to save for a rainy day instead of buying a toy can be a valuable lesson. Explain to your child how saving a portion of their money can provide security for unexpected expenses or allow them to purchase something more meaningful. This choice highlights the importance of foresight and planning, teaching them to prioritize their spending and consider the benefits of saving over time. By illustrating the impact of their choices, you help them see the bigger picture and understand how small decisions can lead to significant outcomes.

Using real-life scenarios can make these lessons more relatable and impactful. Please encourage your child to think about their lunch choice. For example, opting for a homemade lunch instead of buying from the cafeteria can save money to put toward something they've been saving for. This decision teaches them about opportunity cost—choosing one option often means giving up another. By weighing the pros and cons of each choice, they learn to evaluate their options critically and make informed decisions. This skill will benefit them in many areas of life.

Providing tools and strategies for decision-making is crucial. Introduce them to simple tools like pros and cons lists for financial decisions. Please encourage your child to write down the advantages and disadvantages of each choice, helping them visualize their options. This exercise fosters critical thinking and encourages them to consider all angles before deciding. Additionally, they should be taught about financial decision trees, where they can map out the potential outcomes of their choices. This tool helps them see the possible consequences of their actions and make choices that align with their goals and values.

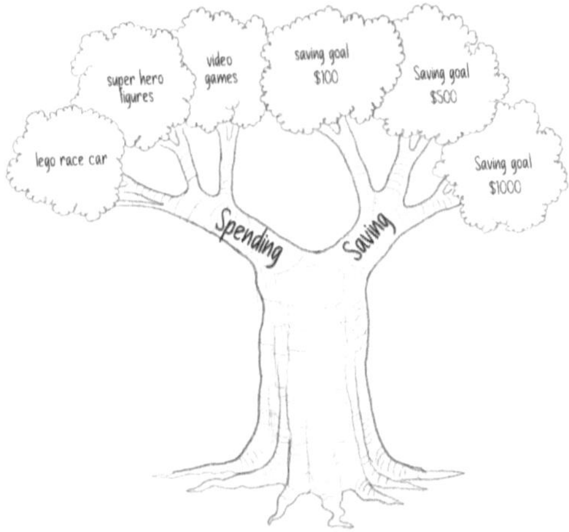

using decision trees can be an engaging and effective way to teach kids about decision-making.

Interactive Exercise: Decision-Making Checklist

Create a decision-making checklist with your child. Start with a situation where they must decide between saving or spending. Work through the checklist together, listing the pros and cons of each option and mapping out potential long-term effects. This interactive exercise engages them in the decision-making process and provides a structured approach to evaluating their choices. By practicing with the checklist, your child gains confidence in their ability to make informed decisions, laying the foundation for responsible financial behavior.

As they navigate the world of financial choices, your child will learn that every decision has a ripple effect. By providing them with the tools to evaluate their options and make thoughtful decisions, you empower them to take charge of their financial future. They begin to see money not just as something to be spent but as a resource to be managed wisely. Through your guidance, they cultivate a mindset of responsibility and foresight, setting the stage for a lifetime of smart financial choices.

THE CONSEQUENCES OF SPENDING: A CAUTIONARY TALE

Meet Charlie, a spirited young boy with a boundless imagination and a knack for spending every penny he gets his hands on. One sunny afternoon, Charlie found himself in possession of his entire savings jar, a collection of coins he'd diligently gathered from weekly allowances and birthday gifts. The world was his oyster; the latest video game was *The Pearl*. Without a second thought, Charlie dashed to the store, his mind set on the thrilling adventures in the game's digital universe.

With the game in hand, Charlie felt triumphant, like a king in his castle. But as the days passed, the excitement began to wane, leaving a lingering feeling of emptiness in his coin jar. It was then that Charlie's parents reminded him of an upcoming school trip to the science museum that promised a day full of learning, fun, and friendship. But there was a catch: Each child needed to bring a small fee for the entrance. Charlie's heart sank as he realized his impulsive spending left him with nothing for the trip, which he had eagerly anticipated.

In this moment of realization, Charlie learned the hard way about the importance of planning and foresight. It dawned on him that his choice to buy the game had consequences, not just on his savings but also on the experiences he could partake in. He wished he had thought it through, perhaps saved a portion for the game and set aside the rest for future adventures like the school trip. Charlie's predicament became a powerful lesson in understanding that spending decisions can have lasting effects, often beyond the immediate gratification of a new toy or game.

Imagine if Charlie had paused before purchasing the game, considering the upcoming trip. He might have chosen to save part of his money, ensuring he could enjoy the game and still join his friends at the museum. This decision point highlights the value of budgeting and setting priorities. By weighing his options and considering future events, Charlie could have avoided the disappointment and gained a sense of accomplishment in managing his finances wisely. This alternative outcome demonstrates that with some planning, children can enjoy their current desires while preparing for future needs.

The moral of Charlie's story is clear. While spending can be tempting and fun at the moment, it's crucial to think ahead and consider the bigger picture. Planning and setting priorities help avoid the pitfalls of impulsive spending, allowing children to enjoy their wants and needs thoroughly. By learning to budget and save, they gain the freedom to participate in opportunities that arise, whether it's a school trip, a new hobby, or even a chance to help others. This foresight is a cornerstone of financial literacy, teaching children that smart choices today pave the way for a fulfilling tomorrow.

Through Charlie's tale, children can see the importance of managing their money with care and thoughtfulness. It's a reminder that financial decisions are not just about the present but also about the future. By keeping their eyes on the horizon and planning accordingly, they can make the most of their resources and enjoy the adventures life has to offer. This story becomes a guide, showing them how to navigate the world of spending with wisdom and responsibility, ensuring they are always ready for the joys and challenges that come their way.

GIVING BACK: SHARING AND CHARITY

Picture a Saturday morning when your child is sorting through their toys, deciding which ones they still play with and which have been forgotten in the corner. This moment can become a powerful lesson in sharing and charity, transforming it into an opportunity to teach them about giving back. Explain to your child that sharing a portion of what they have can make a real difference in someone else's life. It could be as simple as donating a portion of their allowance to a local charity or choosing a few toys to give to children who might not have as much. This act of giving teaches them that financial responsibility isn't only about managing one's money but also about using it to help others. It instills a sense of empathy and community, reminding them that we all have the power to contribute positively to the world around us.

An undeniable joy comes from helping others, and children can feel this deeply. By donating their allowance or participating in charitable activities, they experience a sense of fulfillment that goes beyond the material. They learn that giving can be as rewarding, if not more so, than receiving. It helps them develop a broader perspective, seeing beyond their immediate wants to the needs of others. This understanding fosters a mindset of gratitude and generosity, invaluable qualities as they grow into adulthood. By encouraging your child to give back, you nurture their ability to empathize and connect with the community, strengthening their social and emotional development.

Engaging your child in philanthropic activities can be both educational and fun. Consider organizing a toy drive where your child can take the lead in collecting toys from friends and neighbors to donate to a local shelter. Or, participate in a charity walk together to learn about raising funds for a cause they care about. These activities provide hands-on experiences that teach the importance of teamwork and community involvement. They also allow your child to see their efforts' direct impact, reinforcing their contributions' value. Through these experiences, they gain confidence in their ability to make a difference, learning that even small acts of kindness can significantly impact those in need.

Children have an incredible capacity for compassion and creativity, and stories of young philanthropists can serve as powerful inspiration. Take, for instance, the tale of Delilah

Schoonover, a six-year-old who collected quarters all summer and donated $150 in coins to Habitat Tucson, believing that all kids should have a home. Her story is a testament to the impact that even the youngest among us can have when they set their minds to helping others.

Sharing these stories with your child may inspire them to embark on their own charitable projects. Encourage them to think about what causes matter most and how they can use their resources, time, or talents to support those causes. This exploration fosters a sense of agency and purpose, empowering them to act on their values and make a tangible difference in their community. Through these experiences, your child learns that financial responsibility extends beyond personal gain, encompassing a commitment to giving back and supporting others. They see first-hand that their contributions, no matter how small, are valuable and appreciated, reinforcing the idea that everyone has the power to make a positive impact.

THE POWER OF PLANNING: SETTING FINANCIAL PRIORITIES

Imagine a day at the park with your child, where they eagerly look across the playground, considering whether to spend their allowance on ice cream or save for a new toy they've had their eye on. This seemingly simple scenario is a perfect way to introduce the concept of financial prioritization. It's about teaching children to distinguish between immediate needs and long-term goals, like choosing between ice cream's instant sweetness and a cherished toy's lasting joy. Helping them understand this distinction lays the groundwork for effective resource allocation, ensuring they can enjoy the present and the future without regret.

Planning plays a pivotal role in achieving better financial outcomes. It opens up possibilities by turning vague dreams into achievable goals. For your child, this might mean creating a savings plan for something special, like a new bike or a family outing. By setting aside a small portion of their weekly allowance, they learn the value of discipline and the satisfaction of reaching a goal through thoughtful planning. This practice teaches them that even modest contributions can accumulate over time, leading to significant achievements. It's a lesson in patience and perseverance, showing them that the rewards of planning are well worth the wait.

To support your child in setting financial priorities, provide them with practical tools and techniques. Introduce planners or financial apps designed specifically for kids, as these can make planning engaging and accessible. These tools often feature colorful interfaces and fun elements that appeal to young minds, helping them track their savings and spending in a user-friendly way. Through these resources, your child can visualize their progress and adjust their plans as needed, making the abstract concept of financial planning tangible and interactive. This hands-on approach reinforces their understanding and empowers them to take control of their finances, fostering independence and confidence.

Engaging in planning exercises can further solidify these skills. Consider role-playing a scenario where your child is tasked with planning a budget for their upcoming birthday party. Discuss the elements, from decorations and snacks to entertainment and party favors. Please encourage them to list their priorities and allocate their budget accordingly, making choices that align with their vision for the celebration. This exercise allows them to practice setting and adjusting priorities in a real-world context, providing a safe space to experiment and learn. As they navigate the planning process, they gain valuable insights into resource management and decision-making, skills that will serve them well throughout their lives.

In teaching your child the power of planning and prioritization, you equip them with the tools to navigate their financial future with wisdom and foresight. They begin to see money not just as something to be spent impulsively but as a resource to be managed carefully and thoughtfully. Through your guidance, they learn that with some planning and prioritization, they can achieve their goals and enjoy the journey along the way.

LEARNING FROM FAMILY: FINANCIAL LESSONS AT HOME

Picture a cozy evening at home, where dinner has just been cleared, and the family gathers around the table for a chat. This setting is perfect for sharing financial wisdom, where everyday conversations can spark a lifetime of learning. Families are affluent with experience, and children can gain valuable insights by simply asking their parents about budgeting methods or how they manage household expenses. Please encourage your child to be curious about how money flows in and out of their home. They might be surprised to learn how decisions are made about paying bills, saving for vacations, or planning unexpected expenses. This dialogue educates them and strengthens family bonds, creating a safe space where financial topics can be discussed openly and honestly.

Family discussing budgeting and savings after dinner

Family stories and experiences serve as powerful tools for imparting financial wisdom. Imagine sharing a tale about a grandparent who saved diligently for a special gift, teaching the value of patience and perseverance. Such stories bring economic concepts to life, illustrating the impact of wise decisions and hard work. It could be a story of how your parents saved for a family trip or the first home. These anecdotes provide a glimpse into the past, revealing how financial responsibility shaped the lives of those who came before. By connecting these tales to real-life outcomes, children can better understand the importance of managing money wisely and the rewards that come with it.

Consider introducing family financial activities as a fun and educational way to learn about money together. Organize a family budgeting night where everyone can plan the monthly expenses. This activity involves each family member, allowing them to contribute ideas and insights. It's a chance for children to see firsthand how financial decisions are made and to understand the importance of collaboration and communication in managing household finances. You might also host a home finance workshop, where family members can take turns presenting on different financial topics, like saving strategies or understanding interest rates. These activities demystify financial concepts and encourage teamwork and shared responsibility.

Family dynamics play a significant role in shaping financial habits. Children often observe and mimic the spending patterns and attitudes toward money they see at home. If they see their parents budgeting carefully and discussing financial matters openly, they are more likely to adopt similar practices. Creating an environment where financial education is part of everyday life, questions are welcomed, and continuous learning is essential. By fostering a culture of financial awareness, you empower your children to develop healthy money habits that will serve them well into adulthood. Please encourage them to participate in discussions about family spending habits, whether deciding on a family outing or choosing between wants and needs.

Through these family interactions, children learn that financial education is not confined to textbooks or classrooms but is woven into the fabric of daily life. They discover that their family is a valuable resource, offering insights and lessons beyond mere numbers. By engaging with family stories, activities, and discussions, they gain a deeper appreciation for money's role in their lives and the importance of managing it wisely. These lessons provide a foundation for financial literacy, equipping them with the knowledge and skills to navigate their financial futures confidently and clearly.

THE IMPORTANCE OF HONESTY IN MONEY MATTERS

Honesty in financial dealings is like the sturdy foundation of a house. Without it, everything else risks crumbling. Teaching kids the value of honesty when it comes to money is crucial. It starts with being truthful about their spending and saving habits. Imagine your child has a piggy bank where they've been diligently saving for a new toy. One day, they decide to take out a bit more than planned to buy a comic book, promising they'll replace it soon. Suppose they don't acknowledge this to themselves or you. In that case, it might become a habit, undermining their ability to reach their goals. Encouraging them to be honest about these moments, even if they feel small, helps them understand the importance of integrity. It's about creating an environment where transparency is valued, allowing them to learn and grow from their decisions.

Honesty extends beyond personal habits to include financial transactions and agreements with others. Consider a simple trip to the corner store where your child accidentally receives extra change. This presents a perfect opportunity to teach them about ethical behavior. Returning the additional change, even when no one is looking, reinforces the lesson that integrity matters. It's not just about doing the right thing; it's about building trust and respect in relationships. These small acts of honesty can have a ripple effect, influencing their interactions and creating a reputation for reliability. Kids learn that honesty in transactions fosters trust, whether they're dealing with family, friends, or strangers. By valuing truthfulness in these moments, they lay the groundwork for strong ethical standards.

Real-life examples can illustrate how honesty in money matters impacts relationships. Take the story of Mia and her best friend, Alex. One day, Alex borrowed money from Mia to buy supplies for a school project, promising to pay her back the following week. When the time came, Alex was honest about forgetting to bring the money. He explained his situation, and Mia appreciated his openness. Their friendship grew stronger because of this honesty, as Mia saw Alex as someone she could trust. This story highlights the importance of integrity and how truthfulness can strengthen bonds. Kids learn that honesty is not just a moral value but a practical one that can enhance their relationships. It teaches them that being upfront about financial dealings fosters mutual respect and understanding.

Role-playing scenarios can be an effective way to demonstrate the importance of honesty in financial situations. Set up a simple scenario where one child borrows money from another. Please encourage them to act out both returning the money on time and forgetting to do so. Discuss how each scenario feels and what the consequences might be for their relationship. This exercise makes the concept of honesty more relatable and allows them to explore the emotions and outcomes involved. By engaging in role-play, kids can better understand the impact of their actions, building empathy and reinforcing the value of integrity. It's a safe space for them to experience the importance of honesty and see how it leads to trust and respect.

As we wrap up this chapter, remember that honesty in money matters is the foundation upon which financial responsibility is built. It encourages trust and integrity, which are essential for strong relationships and sound financial habits. By teaching children to be truthful in their financial dealings, we equip them with the tools to navigate the world confidently and clearly. This chapter closes on the idea that honesty is not just a virtue but a practical skill that can open doors and strengthen bonds. As we move forward, we'll explore how these skills translate into the broader world of financial literacy, helping kids become savvy and responsible individuals.

6

MODERN MONEY CONCEPTS

Imagine for a moment that you're at a bustling amusement park with your child. People are zipping past everywhere you look, enjoying rides and snacks without a single bill or coin. Instead, they wave their phones or tap cards to pay. This might seem like magic, but it's the power of digital money in action. Welcome to the world of e-wallets, where cash and coins are replaced by a tap or a swipe. As technology advances, e-wallets are becoming a regular part of our financial landscape, offering a convenient and secure way to handle money without needing physical currency. For kids growing up in this digital age, understanding e-wallets is just as important as knowing how to count change.

E-wallets, or digital wallets, are like virtual versions of the wallets you carry in your pocket. They allow you to store money digitally and make payments without cash or physical cards. Think of them as a personal financial hub on your smartphone, where you can keep everything from credit card information to digital coupons. Famous examples include PayPal and Apple Pay, which you might have already encountered daily. These e-wallets are designed to make transactions smoother and faster, letting you pay for groceries, shop online, or even split a restaurant bill with friends with just a few taps. It's like having a super-powered wallet that keeps track of your spending while staying safely tucked away in your device.

One of the major perks of using e-wallets is the convenience they offer. Imagine making a quick purchase while juggling grocery bags and a squirming toddler. With an e-wallet, you can tap your phone and be on your way. No need to fumble for cash or cards, making the whole process hassle-free. Beyond convenience, e-wallets also bring a layer of security to your transactions. They use encryption to protect your financial information, reducing the risk of theft or fraud. Some e-wallets even offer the ability to track and categorize your spending, helping you stay on top of your finances. This combination of ease and security makes e-wallets an attractive option for families looking to simplify their money management.

Setting up an e-wallet is a straightforward process, and many apps are designed to be user-friendly, even for beginners. Start by choosing an e-wallet that suits your needs, such as Apple Pay for Apple device users or PayPal for a versatile option. Download the app and follow the on-screen instructions to create an account. You'll need to link a payment method, like a bank account or credit card, which is usually a simple process involving a few verification steps. Once your e-wallet is set up, you can make purchases, send money to friends, or store digital tickets and coupons.

It's like setting up a digital assistant for your finances, ready to help immediately.

Paying for groceries via e-Wallets make transactions smoother and faster.

To help your child grasp the concept of e-wallets:

1. Consider engaging them in a fun role-playing activity. You can create a pretend store at home with items for "sale" and a toy cash register.
2. Give your child a pretend e-wallet, a smartphone with a simple app, or a piece of paper representing digital money.
3. Let them "buy" items from the store using their e-wallet, practicing selecting items, confirming purchases, and managing their digital funds.

This interactive play makes learning about e-wallets engaging and gives them a practical understanding of how digital transactions work. It's a playful way to introduce them to the future of money management, helping them build the skills they'll need in a world where digital payments are becoming the norm. Through this hands-on experience, your child will gain confidence in handling digital transactions and be ready to embrace the modern money concepts shaping our financial future.

THE WORLD OF ONLINE SHOPPING: STAYING SAFE

Imagine it's a rainy afternoon, and your child is curled up on the couch, browsing their favorite online store. The virtual aisles are filled with colorful toys and gadgets, just a click away. This is the essence of online shopping, where you can buy almost anything without leaving home. Platforms like Amazon have made it incredibly convenient to find what you need, whether it's a new book for bedtime stories or the latest toy your child has been eyeing. Online shopping opens up a universe of possibilities. Still, it's essential to navigate it safely, ensuring that every purchase is secure and thoughtful.

Teaching your child about safe online shopping begins with identifying secure websites. Encourage them to look for URLs starting with "https://" and a padlock icon in the address bar, symbols of a secure connection. Explain that these features help protect their personal information from falling into the wrong hands. It's also crucial to emphasize the importance of using strong, unique passwords for each online account. A good password should mix letters, numbers, and special characters, making it hard for anyone else to guess. Just like you wouldn't use the same key for your house and car, using different passwords for different sites adds an extra layer of security.

Encourage your kids to look for URLs starting with https:// and a padlock icon in the address bar.

One way to reinforce these lessons is through simulated shopping experiences. Create a fun activity where your child can practice safe online shopping. Start by helping them make a shopping list of pretend items they want to buy, such as a virtual pet or a new game. Then, guide them through "checking out" on a mock website, ensuring they review each step for security. Discuss why it's essential to read item descriptions and prices carefully, just as they would in real life. This exercise makes the concept of online shopping tangible. It empowers them to make intelligent decisions when they eventually shop for real.

Parental supervision is critical for online shopping, especially for younger children. Encourage your child to always discuss potential purchases with you before clicking the "buy" button. This practice protects them from impulse buying and opens the door to meaningful conversations about money management and priorities. It's an opportunity to guide them in making informed choices, teaching them to balance their wants and needs. By involving them in the decision-making process, you help them develop a sense of responsibility and independence, preparing them for more complex financial decisions as they grow.

Reflection Section: Safe Shopping Checklist

Create a safe shopping checklist with your child. Include items like verifying website security, using strong passwords, and discussing purchases with a parent. Please encourage them to check off each item as they practice their shopping skills, reinforcing the importance of each step. This checklist is a handy reminder, helping them build habits prioritizing safety and intelligent spending. As they grow more comfortable with online shopping, they'll carry these lessons, navigating the digital marketplace with confidence and care.

EXPLORING CRYPTOCURRENCIES: WHAT KIDS SHOULD KNOW

Imagine explaining money to your child, but instead of coins and bills, you describe numbers on a screen. That's essentially what cryptocurrencies are—digital or virtual currencies that don't exist in a physical form. They use cryptography, a fancy term for secret codes, to secure transactions. Bitcoin is the most well-known example and is often what people picture when they think of cryptocurrency. It's like a pioneer in a new frontier of digital finance, representing a shift in how we think about money. Unlike traditional currency, Bitcoin and its counterparts are decentralized, meaning no single entity like a bank or government controls them. This new way of managing money is fascinating. However, it comes with challenges and learning curves that even adults still figure out.

Now, let's talk about how these cryptocurrencies work, and for that, we need to introduce a concept called blockchain technology. Picture a digital ledger, much like an electronic notebook, where every transaction is noted down. This isn't just any ledger, though—it's decentralized and distributed across many computers worldwide. Each page in this ledger is a "block," when linked together, they form a "chain"—hence the name blockchain. This technology ensures that every transaction is transparent and cannot be altered once recorded, making it secure and trustworthy. For kids, you might compare it to a digital diary where every entry is locked and can't be edited once written, ensuring the honesty of the records.

Blockchain described as a ledger entry for kids to understand.

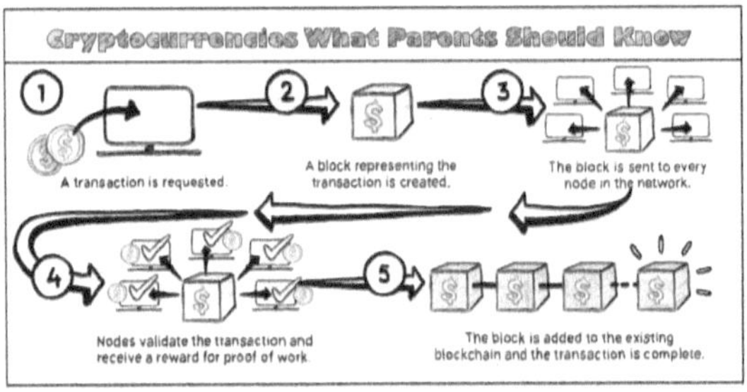

Simple blockchain explanation for parents to understand.

However, a critical aspect of cryptocurrencies is their volatility. Unlike the money in your wallet, which retains its value from day to day, the value of cryptocurrencies can fluctuate wildly. Imagine a roller coaster ride—one day, your Bitcoin might be worth a fortune, and it could drop significantly the next. This is due to various factors, including market demand and economic events, which can lead to rapid changes in value. To illustrate this concept to children, you might use a simple graph showing the ups and downs of cryptocurrency prices over a week. This visual representation can help them understand that investing in cryptocurrencies involves risks, as values can change unpredictably, much like weather patterns.

Cryptocurrencies like Bitcoin can fluctuate wildly from day to day.

To make these concepts more accessible and engaging for children:

1. Consider an interactive activity where they can create a pretend cryptocurrency wallet.
2. Start with a simple app or even a paper version where they can "deposit" pretend cryptocurrencies. As they engage with this activity, you can simulate changes in the value of their holdings to demonstrate volatility.
3. Encourage them to keep track of these ups and downs, helping them understand how their "investment" value changes over time.

This hands-on experience makes learning about cryptocurrencies fun and introduces them to the dynamics of digital finance. Through this playful approach, children can appreciate the complexities and possibilities of cryptocurrencies, preparing them for a future where digital currencies become a more regular part of everyday life.

THE STORY OF OLIVER'S ONLINE ADVENTURE

Oliver was buzzing with excitement. His birthday money burned a hole in his pocket, and he was eager to make his first online purchase. He'd been eyeing a new puzzle game all his friends were discussing. With his parents' guidance, he sat at the family computer, ready to dive into online transactions. His dad reminded him to be cautious and told him about essential steps before buying anything online. Oliver listened carefully, eager to learn how to shop safely and confidently.

As Oliver navigated the website, his dad pointed out the small padlock icon in the address bar, explaining that it meant the site was secure. This little detail was crucial, his dad said, because it protected their personal information while shopping. Oliver felt like a detective, scanning the site for clues to ensure it was safe. He learned to look for "https://" in the web address, a sign that the website was trustworthy. With each new piece of information, Oliver grew more confident in his ability to shop smartly and securely.

The moment came for Oliver to make a choice. He stumbled upon another site offering the same game at a lower price. It looked tempting, but something seemed off. The site lacked the familiar security symbols, and his dad advised caution. Oliver had to decide: go for the cheaper option or stick with the secure site? He weighed the risks, remembering what his dad had taught him about the importance of safety over savings. Ultimately, Oliver chose the secure site, valuing peace of mind over a small discount. It was a decision that made him proud, knowing he prioritized safety.

Throughout this adventure, Oliver learned valuable lessons about online transactions. He discovered the importance of staying informed and cautious. By making smart choices, he protected himself from potential pitfalls. His dad praised his decision-making, emphasizing understanding and respecting online financial tools. Oliver realized that being careful online wasn't just about following rules but taking control of his financial safety. This experience was empowering, turning what might have been a simple purchase into an opportunity for growth and learning.

Oliver's journey continued after the purchase. His dad pointed out the transaction receipt, showing him how to keep records of his online activities. This step was crucial for tracking his spending and spotting any unusual charges. Oliver felt like he was part of a secret club, equipped with knowledge to guide him in future online adventures. He understood that being cautious and informed was vital to enjoying the benefits of digital transactions while staying safe. As he held his new game in hand, Oliver couldn't wait to share his newfound wisdom with his friends, eager to help them confidently navigate their online experiences.

THE FUTURE OF MONEY: TRENDS AND INSIGHTS

It's an exciting time to think about the future of money, especially with how things are changing so quickly. One of the most noticeable trends is the rise of contactless payments and mobile banking. Imagine walking into a store, grabbing what you need, and simply waving your phone or card at the checkout to pay. You're done with no cash or coins—just a quick tap. This technology makes transactions faster and more convenient, especially when managing a busy schedule and having little ones in tow. Mobile banking takes this further, letting you manage your finances from anywhere, whether at the park with your kids or waiting in line at the coffee shop. With a few taps, you can check your balance, transfer money, or even pay bills without stepping foot in a bank.

Some countries are moving toward a cashless society, where physical money is becoming less common. Places like Sweden and China are leading the way, with many businesses preferring digital payments over cash. Even small transactions, like coffee buying, are done digitally in these societies. Imagine a world where your kids grow up without ever having to count change or worry about losing a dollar bill. While cash will be around, the convenience of digital payments is undoubtedly making it less necessary. This shift means learning new ways to think about and handle money for children, preparing them for a world where digital transactions are the norm.

Technology is not just changing how we pay; it's also transforming the very structure of financial systems. Take intelligent contracts, for example. These are like digital agreements that automatically execute once certain conditions are met, eliminating the need for a middleman. Imagine selling a bike online and having an intelligent contract to ensure that the money is transferred as soon as the bike is delivered—no hassle, no waiting. Artificial intelligence (AI) also makes financial waves, helping banks and businesses analyze data, detect fraud, and offer personalized financial advice. These advancements mean that tomorrow's economic landscape will be more efficient and secure, with technology playing a central role in how we handle money. Teaching kids about these innovations can spark their curiosity and prepare them for future possibilities.

To help children engage with these futuristic trends, consider an activity where they can design their own wallets. Please provide them with art supplies or a simple digital design tool and encourage them to think creatively about their wallet's features. Could it track spending automatically? It could suggest savings goals based on their habits. This exercise makes the concept of a cashless society tangible. It encourages kids to think about how they interact with money differently. As they design, they can explore what features would make managing money easier or more fun. This creative process helps them visualize and adapt to the evolution of financial tools, ensuring they're ready for whatever the future holds.

With these insights into the future of money, kids can imagine a world where financial interactions are seamless, efficient, and integrated into everyday life. As parents, guiding them through these changes can be educational and exciting, opening up discussions about how technology shapes our lives and what possibilities lie ahead. In this ever-evolving financial world, staying informed and adaptable will empower children to navigate the changes confidently and creatively.

THE IMPORTANCE OF CYBERSECURITY IN FINANCE

In today's digital age, where almost every financial transaction can happen online, cybersecurity is like the invisible armor that protects our personal information. Think of it as a shield that keeps your data safe from the prying eyes of cybercriminals. Cybersecurity involves practices designed to protect your electronic information from unauthorized access and cyber threats. Just as you teach your child to look both ways before crossing the street, it's essential to instill the basics of cybersecurity to ensure their online activities remain secure. This means keeping personal data, like passwords and bank details, out of reach from those who might misuse it.

Cyber threats, unfortunately, are all too common and can impact financial security significantly. Phishing scams, for instance, are a popular tactic where scammers pretend to be trustworthy entities to trick you into giving away sensitive information. Imagine receiving an email that looks like it's from your bank, asking you to update your password. It seems legitimate, but it could be a scam to steal your data. Another threat is identity theft, where someone illegally uses your personal information to commit fraud. These digital dangers are invisible traps with real-world consequences if not carefully navigated. Teaching your child about these threats is crucial so they understand the importance of being cautious online.

There are practical cybersecurity tips that you and your child can follow. One of the most effective measures is using two-factor authentication (2FA), which adds an extra layer of security by requiring a second form of verification, like a text message code, before accessing an account. It's like having two locks on a door instead of one. Additionally, encourage your child to recognize and avoid suspicious emails by looking for red flags, such as poor grammar, urgent requests, or unfamiliar sender addresses. These emails often try to create a sense of panic, urging quick action without thinking, so it's essential to teach kids to pause and evaluate before clicking any links or attachments.

Engaging children in cybersecurity simulations can make these concepts more tangible and fun. Create a game at home where you simulate a phishing attempt. You can send a pretend email or message from a "bank" to your child, asking for their "password." When they respond, use the opportunity to explain why it was a phishing attempt and what signs they should look out for in real scenarios. This interactive approach makes learning about cyber threats engaging and empowers them to apply these lessons in real life. Through these activities, children learn to develop a critical eye, questioning and analyzing online information.

As we wrap up this chapter on modern money concepts, remember that cybersecurity is not just a technical necessity but a crucial life skill in today's digital world. It's about instilling a mindset of caution and awareness, ensuring you and your child can navigate the online world safely. By understanding the landscape of digital threats and the tools available to combat them, you're setting the stage for a financially secure future. With these skills, your child will be better equipped to handle tomorrow's financial challenges, blending the security of the past with future innovations. The next chapter explores how these modern concepts integrate with personal responsibility and savvy financial habits.

7

ENGAGING WITH MONEY THROUGH TECHNOLOGY

In today's digital age, technology is transforming how children learn about money. Picture your child sitting at the kitchen table, tablet in hand, immersed in an educational finance app. These apps do more than display numbers; they create vibrant worlds where financial concepts come alive through interactive play. With various apps designed for young learners, understanding money has never been more enjoyable and accessible. They make learning about budgeting, saving, and investing engaging and relatable.

Popular Financial Apps for Kids

There are numerous apps tailored to teach children about money management. Here are two standout examples:

- **Greenlight:** This app allows children to track their spending, manage their allowance, and even learn about investing. Kids can create savings goals and see their progress, turning financial lessons into engaging activities.

- **PiggyBot:** This app helps kids visualize their savings and spending goals, making it easy to manage allowances effectively. Children can allocate funds for different purposes, reinforcing the idea of budgeting in a fun and interactive way.

These tools help children actively engage and apply financial concepts, making learning feel like an adventure. Interactive lessons and quizzes embed essential skills while retaining their interest.

Choosing the Right App

When selecting a financial app for your child, consider the following:

- Research: Check app reviews and ratings to ensure effectiveness and reliability. Look for parent feedback to gauge success.
- Parental Controls: Opt for apps that offer features allowing you to monitor your child's progress, ensuring a safe learning environment. Be cautious of in-app purchases and data privacy.
- Age Appropriateness: Select apps that align with your child's age and learning style to prevent frustration while keeping them engaged.

App Exploration Activities

Engaging your child with app exploration enhances their learning experience. Encourage them to test different features of a chosen app, such as setting up a pretend budget or tracking a savings goal. This hands-on exploration reinforces their understanding of financial concepts and shows them how technology can aid in money management.

Interactive Activity: App Exploration Checklist

Create a checklist to guide your child in using a new financial app. Include tasks such as:

- Setting a savings goal
- Tracking expenses
- Completing a quiz or lesson

Encourage them to check off each item as they complete tasks, providing a sense of accomplishment and motivation. This checklist helps them understand the app's potential effectively.

Gamifying Finance: Fun With Learning Games

Gamifying financial education turns learning into a playful adventure. By incorporating elements of games, we can engage children in budgeting and saving activities that feel exciting rather than educational chores.

Popular games like **Budgeting Bonanza** and **Savings Safari** make learning about money management enjoyable. In Budgeting Bonanza, kids navigate a colorful board, making strategic choices about spending and saving as they work toward their financial goals. Savings Safari takes children on an adventure where they earn rewards for wise resource management.

Encouraging Effective Learning

The thrill of earning points or badges for achieving savings goals keeps children motivated. Setting small, attainable goals within the game fosters a sense of achievement similar to leveling up in a video game. Not only are they learning about finances, but they're also developing strategic thinking and discipline.

To engage them further, challenge your child to design their own financial game. This activity taps into their creativity while deepening their understanding. They can build a board game where players earn and spend money or create a digital game that teaches financial concepts. Involving them in the game design process enables them to think critically about what they've learned, turning abstract ideas into interactive experiences.

DIGITAL BUDGETING APPS FOR YOUNG SAVERS

Budgeting apps for kids, such as Allowance & Chores Bot, provide an interactive platform for children to easily learn how to create and manage their budgets. These tools allow kids to allocate their allowance, track their spending, and set savings goals while making the learning experience enjoyable.

Key Features of Budgeting Apps:

- **User-Friendly Interfaces:** Colorful graphics and intuitive designs help children visualize financial habits, showing where money comes from and where it goes.
- **Visual Representations:** Many apps include pie charts and graphs, helping kids understand their income and expenses at a glance. For instance, they can see how much they've spent on toys versus how much they've saved for a bike.
- **Goal Setting and Progress Tracking:** Children can monitor their savings over time, experiencing a sense of accomplishment as they approach their financial targets.
- **Interactive Elements:** Engaging gamified components turn budgeting from a chore into an exciting activity, motivating kids to stick to their budgets and make thoughtful financial decisions.

Getting the Most from Budgeting Apps:

- **Set Realistic Goals:** Encourage your child to start small, perhaps saving for a toy or a special outing. Help them break down their goals into manageable steps, such as allocating a portion of their weekly allowance.
- **Regular Budget Check-Ins:** Schedule time to review their app together, discussing successes and

areas for improvement. This reinforces lessons learned and promotes meaningful conversations about money management.

- **Introduce Budgeting Challenges:** Create friendly competitions where your child aims to save a specific amount within a month. Offering small rewards for achieving their goals adds motivation and enhances their financial literacy through fun.

By leveraging these budgeting apps, children can develop a sense of responsibility and ownership over their financial choices, building confidence in managing money effectively. They learn that budgeting is not merely about restriction; it's about making informed decisions that align with their goals and values.

TECH-SAVVY KIDS: NAVIGATING FINANCIAL TOOLS

Picture a world where your child can navigate online banking platforms as quickly as they scroll through their favorite cartoon apps. Understanding and using financial technology is becoming increasingly important, even for our youngest learners. In today's digital age, being tech-savvy is not just a bonus; it's a necessity. Kids who grow up comfortable with technology will find it easier to manage their finances as they age. They can use online banking platforms to check balances, transfer funds, and even pay allowances digitally. This familiarity builds a foundation of confidence and independence, empowering them to take charge of their own financial well-being.

Essential digital financial tools provide a helpful introduction to managing money. Online calculators, for example, are fantastic for teaching children about interest and savings. These digital tools allow kids to input numbers and see how their savings could grow over time with interest. Imagine your child entering how much they've saved in their piggy bank and then watching as the calculator shows the potential growth over the years. It's like turning abstract numbers into a visual story of their financial future. This hands-on experience demystifies the concept of interest, making it accessible and engaging. Using these tools, children can experiment and learn without fearing making mistakes, building their confidence in handling money.

While digital tools are handy, teaching responsible use is crucial. Kids need to understand the importance of protecting their personal information online. Just like you wouldn't share your home address with a stranger, children should learn to keep their login details and personal data private. This means using strong, unique passwords and being cautious about which sites they enter their information on. It's about fostering a sense of vigilance and care, ensuring they grow up with a healthy respect for their digital footprint. Teaching them to recognize phishing attempts, like spotting a wolf in sheep's clothing, empowers them to navigate the internet safely. This responsibility instills a sense of security, reinforcing that they have the tools to protect themselves.

Engaging children with tool exploration activities can make learning about financial tools interactive and fun. Consider setting up a small exercise where your child simulates a transaction using a digital tool. For example, they can pretend to buy a toy online using a mock banking app. Guide them through checking their "balance," entering their "payment details," and confirming the purchase. This activity teaches them how transactions work and introduces them to the idea of digital banking. They learn to handle each step carefully, understanding the flow of money and the importance of accuracy. This hands-on approach transforms learning into an adventure, making complex concepts easy to grasp.

Tool Exploration Worksheet

Create a worksheet that guides your child through exploring a digital financial tool. Include steps like logging in, checking balances, and simulating a transaction. Please encourage them to share their observations and thoughts as they complete each step. This worksheet acts as a roadmap, helping them confidently navigate the tool. As they work through it, they'll gain a deeper understanding of how digital tools aid in managing money, equipping them with skills they can carry into adulthood.

THE ROLE OF TECHNOLOGY IN SHAPING FINANCIAL FUTURES

Imagine a world where your child can pay for a snack with digital currency, all with a simple tap on their smartwatch. Digital currencies like Bitcoin and Ethereum are becoming more prevalent, representing a shift from traditional money to virtual forms of currency. These digital currencies use blockchain technology—a secure and transparent digital ledger that records transactions. Blockchain technology isn't just a buzzword; it's a revolutionary way of handling information securely. For kids growing up in this era, understanding these advancements is as crucial as knowing how to save their allowance in a piggy bank. As these technologies evolve, they hold the potential to transform our financial landscape, making transactions faster and more secure while also introducing new ways to invest and save.

The future of personal finance could be drastically different, with its increased automation playing a central role. Picture a world where financial management is largely automated, with intelligent algorithms handling everything from budgeting to investing. Instead of manually tracking expenses, families could rely on smart systems that categorize and analyze spending patterns, offering personalized advice on saving and investing more wisely. This automation could simplify financial tasks, freeing time for more meaningful activities. For children, this means growing up in an environment where managing money is seamlessly integrated into their daily lives, much like using a smartphone today. Adapting to these changes will be critical as technology continues to reshape how we interact with our finances.

Adapting to technological changes requires a willingness to learn and grow. As new financial tools and trends emerge, it's essential to cultivate a mindset of continuous learning. Encourage your child to explore and stay curious about the latest advancements in financial technology. This could involve reading about new apps, experimenting with digital wallets, or learning about emerging investment platforms. By fostering a sense of adaptability, children can become comfortable with change and develop the skills needed to navigate an ever-evolving financial landscape. This adaptability will serve them well in managing their finances and other areas of life that require flexibility and resilience.

To help children prepare for future financial technologies, consider engaging them in activities that encourage forward-thinking and creativity. Brainstorm potential future financial tools and their uses together. What might banking look like in 10 or 20 years? Could a device instantly calculate the best savings plan based on personal spending habits? This exercise stimulates their imagination and helps them envision the possibilities that lie ahead. By thinking about the future, children can develop a proactive approach to learning, stay ahead of the curve, and be ready to embrace new challenges and opportunities. Through these discussions, they gain insight into the role of technology in shaping their financial futures, understanding that being open to change is an asset, not a hindrance.

AUGMENTED REALITY: BRINGING MONEY LESSONS TO LIFE

Picture your child standing in the middle of the living room, wearing sleek augmented reality (AR) glasses that transform their surroundings into a vibrant learning playground. Through these glasses, they can see a virtual piggy bank hovering before their eyes, slowly filling up with coins as they complete tasks and save money. This is the future of financial education, where AR turns intangible concepts into interactive experiences. By using AR, we can make lessons about money as immersive as a video game, where children can visualize the growth of their savings in a way that feels real and engaging. It's like having a personal financial coach guiding them through the steps of smart saving, all within the comfort of their own home.

Augmented Reality.

The beauty of AR lies in its ability to take abstract financial concepts and make them tangible. Imagine your child exploring a 3D model of a bustling economic system, where they can observe how banks, markets, and currencies interact. They can zoom in to see how a simple deposit can ripple through the system or how a stock market operates in real time. This interactive approach does more than explain; it allows children to experience and understand the intricate dance of financial processes. By manipulating these 3D models, they gain a deeper appreciation for the mechanisms behind money, learning through word exploration and experimentation. It's a hands-on way to grasp the complexities of finance, making learning both informative and exciting.

One practical application of AR in financial education is through apps that simulate stock market scenarios. Imagine your child stepping into a virtual stock exchange, where they can buy, sell, and trade stocks in a simulated environment. These apps offer a safe space to experiment with investment strategies, showing how real-time market changes affect stock values. It's like playing a game where the stakes are knowledge and understanding rather than financial loss. By engaging with these simulations, children learn the principles of investing, risk, and reward without the pressure of real-world consequences. This experience builds confidence and curiosity, encouraging them to explore the world of finance with an adventurous spirit.

To further enrich this learning experience, consider engaging your child in AR exploration activities. For example, they could create their AR experience by explaining a budgeting process. Using a simple AR app, they might design a scenario where virtual objects represent different budget categories, such as savings, spending, and sharing. As they interact with these objects, they can move funds from one category to another, observing how their choices affect their overall budget. This activity reinforces budgeting concepts and empowers them to take control of their financial decisions in a dynamic and interactive way. By crafting their AR experiences, children become active participants in their learning, developing creativity and critical thinking.

As we wrap up this chapter, it's clear that technology, significantly augmented reality, is reshaping how we teach financial literacy to the next generation. By making abstract concepts tangible and learning interactive, AR opens up new possibilities for engaging with money in once unimaginable ways. As we look to the future, these tools will play a crucial role in preparing our kids to navigate the complexities of the financial world with confidence and curiosity.

8

EMPOWERMENT THROUGH FINANCIAL KNOWLEDGE

Picture a day at the beach with your child, where each grain of sand represents a piece of knowledge that builds the foundation of a sandcastle. Just as every grain adds strength to the structure, every bit of financial knowledge your child gains fortifies their confidence and independence in managing money. Empowering them with the right information can transform uncertainty into self-assurance, allowing them to navigate financial waters with ease. This chapter focuses on building that confidence by helping your child understand the basics and make independent financial decisions, setting the stage for a lifetime of smart money management.

Understanding financial concepts can be a game-changer for children, turning what might seem like a daunting task into an adventure of discovery. Knowledge about money reduces fear and uncertainty, much like knowing the rules of a game makes it more enjoyable. When children understand how money works, they feel empowered to make decisions that align with their goals. This confidence stems from knowing that money is not just something to spend but a tool they can control and use wisely. It's about transforming money from a mysterious force into a familiar friend, one they can trust and rely on. As they learn, they'll discover that financial independence is within their reach, and with it comes the freedom to chase their dreams.

Encouraging children to make independent financial decisions is a critical step in building confidence. Start small by allowing them to decide how to spend part of their allowance. This doesn't mean giving them free rein but guiding them with gentle nudges and questions to help them think critically. For example, if they want to buy a new toy, ask them to consider if it's something they truly want or if there might be something else they'd rather save for. This process teaches them to evaluate their choices and prioritize their spending. By giving them the autonomy to make decisions, you're teaching them to trust their judgment and learn from their experiences, whether they're successful or not. It's about letting them experience the joy of making their own decisions and the lessons that come with them.

Financial independence offers a world of opportunities and freedom. When children learn to manage their money wisely, they open doors to new experiences and projects. Take, for instance, a child who saves up for a personal project like building a model airplane or funding a small garden. These endeavors teach them about setting goals and working toward them, fostering a sense of achievement and satisfaction. Financial independence empowers them to take control of their lives, making choices that reflect their values and aspirations. It's about giving them the tools to shape their future and pursue their passions with confidence. This independence is not just about having money but understanding its potential to enhance their lives and the world around them.

To build this independence, provide your child with strategies that make financial decisions more approachable. Practice making choices in safe environments, like a pretend store set up at home. Let them "buy" items using play money, encouraging them to consider their options carefully. This practice helps them become comfortable with the idea of spending and saving, preparing them for real-world scenarios. It's like rehearsing a play before stepping onto the stage, ensuring they're ready to shine when the spotlight is on them. Through these exercises, children learn to navigate their financial landscape with confidence, equipped with the knowledge and skills to make informed decisions.

Interactive Exercise: Financial Reflection Journal

Introduce your child to the idea of a Financial Reflection Journal. Encourage them to jot down their thoughts after making financial decisions, whether it's how they spent their allowance or why they chose to save for a particular item. This exercise helps them reflect on their choices and understand the reasoning behind their decisions. Over time, they'll see patterns in their spending habits and learn what works best for them. This reflection fosters self-awareness and critical thinking, essential components of financial independence. It's a simple yet powerful tool that helps them grow into confident, informed individuals capable of managing their finances with ease and foresight.

ENCOURAGING QUESTIONS: THE CURIOUS SAVER

Imagine an afternoon spent at the kitchen table with your child, surrounded by colorful stickers, markers, and a growing pile of coins. Questions begin to flow naturally as they inspect each shiny piece, perhaps wondering about the faces on the coins or the numbers inscribed. It's in these moments that curiosity is piqued, and as a parent, you have the wonderful opportunity to create a safe space for these inquiries. Encouraging your child to ask questions about money is like opening a door to understanding. It's about fostering an environment where questions are welcomed and explored together without fear of judgment or dismissal. When children feel safe to ask, they learn to see questions as stepping stones to deeper knowledge. This culture of curiosity is vital in nurturing a lifelong interest in financial literacy.

Asking "why" is a powerful tool in a child's learning arsenal. It turns abstract ideas into tangible concepts by inviting them to explore the reasoning behind financial practices. Why do we save money? What happens when we invest? These questions help kids delve into the mechanics of financial choices, transforming them from passive recipients of information to active participants in their own learning. This inquiry-based approach encourages them to think critically and understand the purpose behind actions, fostering a deeper connection with financial principles. By exploring the "why" behind saving and investing, children begin to appreciate the long-term benefits and responsibilities of managing money. They learn that every financial decision has a rationale and potential outcome, which can guide them in making informed choices.

To stimulate this curiosity, consider incorporating activities designed to prompt questions and exploration. A financial scavenger hunt, for example, can be an exciting way to engage your child's curiosity. Create a list of financial items or concepts for them to find around the house, such as a bank statement or a receipt. As they hunt, encourage them to ask what each item is and how it relates to managing money. This activity turns learning into a game, making abstract financial concepts more relatable and understandable. It's about making the process interactive and enjoyable, allowing children to connect the dots between everyday objects and financial literacy. Such activities empower them to take charge of their learning, sparking curiosity that can lead to lifelong financial awareness.

Stories have a magical way of illustrating complex ideas, and sharing tales of curious savers can inspire your child to embrace their own inquisitiveness. Tell them about a young entrepreneur who, fueled by endless questions, transformed a simple idea into a thriving business. This child asked questions at every step, seeking mentors and absorbing knowledge like a sponge. Through curiosity, they learned about budgeting, investing, and growing their venture, leading to financial success. These stories highlight the power of inquiry and learning from others, showing children that curiosity isn't just about seeking answers but also about discovering possibilities. By learning from the experiences of others, children understand that their questions can lead to growth and achievement. They see that asking questions isn't just a way to learn—it's a pathway to innovation and success.

Encouraging questions and fostering a curious mindset equips children with the tools they need to navigate the financial world confidently. It teaches them that it's okay not to have all the answers as long as they're willing to seek them out. This mindset encourages continuous learning and exploration, which are vital skills in a world where financial landscapes are constantly evolving. By nurturing their curiosity, you help them build a solid foundation for making informed financial decisions, now and in the future. As they grow, this inquisitive approach will serve them well, opening doors to new opportunities and empowering them to take control of their financial journeys.

SETTING PERSONAL FINANCIAL GOALS: A ROADMAP

Imagine your child standing in front of a blank canvas, paintbrush in hand, ready to create a masterpiece. Setting personal financial goals is a bit like painting a picture of the future they desire. It's about envisioning what they want to achieve and plotting a course to make it happen. Personal financial goals are crucial for individual growth, as they provide direction and purpose. They give children a sense of ownership over their financial lives, helping them understand that their choices today can shape their tomorrow. Differentiating between personal and family financial goals is essential. Family goals might involve saving for a vacation or a new home, while personal goals could be as simple as saving for a toy or as ambitious as funding a personal project. When children learn to set personal goals, they gain confidence in their ability to influence their own financial outcomes.

Guiding children through the process of goal setting requires a clear roadmap. Start by helping them identify what they truly want to achieve. Encourage them to think about both short-term desires, like a new game or book, and longer-term aspirations, such as a bicycle or a special experience. Once they've identified their goals, the next step is planning. This involves breaking down their goals into manageable steps and determining how much to save each week or month. Tracking progress is equally important. Consider using visual aids like charts or graphs to help them see how their savings grow over time. This visual representation makes the process tangible and keeps them motivated. As they track their progress, they can adjust their plans as needed, learning the importance of flexibility and adaptability in achieving their goals.

Achieving personal goals is a powerful motivator. It boosts confidence and instills a sense of accomplishment. Celebrating small milestones along the way is key to maintaining motivation. Each milestone, whether it's reaching a savings target or making a smart financial decision, is an opportunity to celebrate their progress. These celebrations don't have to be grand; a simple acknowledgment of their hard work can make a big difference. Recognizing their achievements reinforces the idea that their efforts are paying off and encourages them to keep pushing forward. It also teaches them the value of perseverance, showing them that dedication and discipline can lead to success. Through this process, they learn that every step, no matter how small, brings them closer to their dreams.

Engaging children with goal-setting workshops can enhance their understanding and commitment to their financial aspirations. Consider organizing a workshop where they can create and refine their goals. During the workshop, they can participate in activities like vision boarding, where they create a visual collage of their financial dreams and aspirations. This creative exercise encourages them to think about what they truly value and desire. It also provides a platform for discussion, where they can share their goals with others and receive feedback. These workshops foster a sense of community and support, helping children realize they're not alone in their financial journey. They learn from each other, gain new perspectives, and develop a deeper understanding of what it takes to achieve their goals.

As children set and work toward their personal financial goals, they develop essential life skills. They learn to prioritize, plan, and adapt skills that will serve them well beyond financial management. These experiences teach them the importance of setting clear objectives and working diligently to achieve them. They also learn that setbacks are part of the process and that resilience and determination are key to overcoming challenges. By setting personal financial goals, children gain a sense of agency and empowerment. They understand that they have the power to shape their own futures and that, with the right mindset and approach, anything is possible. This empowerment extends beyond finances, influencing other areas of their lives and helping them grow into confident, capable individuals.

THE COMMUNITY OF LEARNERS: SHARING FINANCIAL KNOWLEDGE

Imagine a lively room filled with kids gathered around tables, chattering excitedly as they swap money-saving tips and share stories about their financial adventures. This vibrant scene captures the essence of a peer-led finance club, where children come together to discuss and explore financial concepts with one another. Encouraging kids to share what they learn about finance not only reinforces their own understanding but also creates a ripple effect of knowledge that benefits everyone involved. It's like planting seeds in a garden, where each child contributes their unique knowledge and experiences, helping the entire community grow stronger and more informed.

Kids gathered around talking about money saving tips.

Being part of a learning community enhances the educational experience, offering support and camaraderie. When children engage in group projects or discussions, they gain diverse perspectives and discover new ways of thinking about financial topics. For instance, one child might share an innovative method for saving money, while another could explain how they budget for a special purchase. These exchanges foster an environment of collaborative learning where everyone learns from one another. It's like a potluck dinner where each dish brings its own flavor, and together, they create a feast of ideas and insights that enrich everyone's understanding.

Creating collaborative learning environments provides children with opportunities to teach and learn from each other. Peer-to-peer teaching sessions or workshops can be incredibly effective, as kids often connect with one another in ways that adults might not. Imagine a workshop where children take turns presenting a financial concept they've mastered, like setting a savings goal or understanding the basics of investing. These workshops not only build confidence but also encourage children to articulate their thoughts and share their insights with others. It's an empowering experience that reinforces their knowledge and instills pride in their ability to contribute to the group's learning.

Celebrating the achievements of learning communities highlights the impact of shared knowledge and collaboration. When children reach group savings goals or accomplish financial milestones, it's important to recognize their success. This could be as simple as organizing a small celebration or awarding certificates of achievement. These celebrations serve as a reminder of what can be accomplished when individuals work together toward a common goal. They also inspire children to continue sharing their knowledge and supporting each other, building a sense of unity and purpose within the community. These shared achievements create a foundation of trust and mutual respect, encouraging children to pursue their financial education with enthusiasm and dedication.

CELEBRATING ACHIEVEMENTS: FINANCIAL MILESTONES

Can you imagine the sense of pride on your child's face when they reach a financial goal they've been working toward. Whether it's buying that coveted toy or saving up for a special outing, these moments are worth celebrating. Recognizing individual accomplishments in money management can significantly boost a child's confidence. When they see their efforts acknowledged, it reinforces the value of hard work and perseverance. Consider marking these milestones in a meaningful way—perhaps a certificate of achievement for their first savings goal or a small celebration to honor their dedication. These gestures show your child that you value their efforts and encourage them to continue striving toward their goals. It's like receiving a gold star, a tangible reminder of their success and an incentive to keep reaching for the stars.

Certificate of Achievement

Milestones play a critical role in keeping children motivated and engaged in their financial journey. They serve as checkpoints, providing tangible evidence of progress and achievement. The anticipation of reaching a milestone can drive a child to stay focused and committed. Implementing a reward system can further enhance this motivation. Rewards don't have to be extravagant; even simple acknowledgments like a favorite meal or extra playtime can be powerful incentives. These rewards act as beacons, guiding children toward their financial targets. As they celebrate each milestone, they build momentum, turning small victories into stepping stones for larger achievements. The excitement of reaching one milestone naturally propels them toward the next, fostering a cycle of motivation and success. This cycle not only strengthens their financial habits but also cultivates a sense of accomplishment that extends beyond money management.

Celebrating financial achievements can be a delightful occasion, filled with activities that reinforce the joy of reaching a goal. Organizing a small party or gathering can be a wonderful way to celebrate savings success. Involve your child in the planning process, letting them choose the theme or menu. This participation adds another layer of engagement, making the celebration even more special. Activities like creating a scrapbook of their savings journey or sharing their story with friends and family can enhance the experience. These celebrations not only recognize their hard work but also create lasting memories associated with financial success. They transform financial achievements into cherished moments, adding a personal touch that resonates with your child. Through these celebrations, children learn that financial milestones are not just about the numbers but the experiences and growth they represent.

Sharing stories of financial milestones can inspire children to set and achieve their own goals. Take the story of a young girl who saved diligently for her first bicycle. She started with a small goal: saving her allowance and doing extra chores. Each week, she watched her savings grow, motivated by the vision of riding her new bike. When she finally reached her goal, the sense of accomplishment was immense. This story, like many others, highlights the power of perseverance and the joy of achieving a significant financial milestone. It shows children that, with determination and dedication, they can turn their dreams into reality. These stories serve as powerful reminders that financial success is within their reach, encouraging them to dream big and work hard. As they hear about others' achievements, they see what's possible, sparking their own aspirations and fueling their journey toward financial independence.

THE JOURNEY AHEAD: LIFELONG FINANCIAL LEARNING

Imagine financial education as a river flowing through life, constantly evolving and expanding with new bends and discoveries. The importance of continuous financial education cannot be overstated. As the world changes, so does the landscape of financial knowledge. New technologies, trends, and economic conditions require us to stay informed and adaptable. Introducing this concept to children early instills a mindset of lifelong learning, encouraging them to see finances not as a static subject but as a dynamic field full of opportunities and challenges. By fostering this perspective, you equip them with the resilience needed to navigate the ever-shifting financial terrain. They learn to approach money management with confidence, understanding that learning doesn't stop once they grasp the basics.

Encouraging children to keep exploring new financial topics is akin to giving them a map of uncharted territories. There's always something new to learn, whether it's understanding a fresh financial tool or grasping the implications of a global economic event. Inspire your kids to seek out books, courses, and mentors who can guide them on their quest for knowledge. This continuous exploration keeps their curiosity alive and their skills sharp. It shows them that learning is an ongoing process, not a destination. By seeking new information and experiences, they cultivate a mindset of growth and adaptability. This proactive approach to learning ensures they're well-equipped to handle whatever financial challenges or opportunities the future may present.

Lifelong learning in financial matters leads to better decision-making. It empowers individuals to adapt to new technologies and trends, making informed choices that align with their goals and values. As children grow, they'll encounter various financial scenarios that require them to apply their knowledge thoughtfully. Whether it's deciding on a savings plan, evaluating investment options, or understanding the implications of a changing job market, ongoing education provides the tools they need to make these decisions confidently. It fosters a sense of agency, helping them take charge of their financial future. This empowerment extends beyond finances, promoting critical thinking and problem-solving skills that benefit all areas of life. By embracing lifelong learning, children develop the ability to navigate an increasingly complex world with poise and assurance.

To support this continuous education, provide resources and tools that facilitate lifelong financial learning. Financial literacy websites, apps, and community programs offer valuable insights and practical knowledge. These resources keep information accessible and engaging, adapting to the evolving needs of learners. Encourage your child to explore these platforms, allowing them to tailor their learning experience to their interests and goals. By utilizing these tools, they gain exposure to diverse perspectives and innovative ideas, broadening their understanding of financial concepts. This exposure enhances their ability to think critically and creatively, equipping them to tackle financial challenges with confidence. It's about creating a rich tapestry of learning experiences that inspire growth and resilience.

As Chapter 8 comes to a close, remember the importance of lifelong financial learning and its impact on developing confident, adaptable individuals. The continuous flow of knowledge empowers children to navigate an ever-changing world, preparing them for the financial realities of tomorrow.

GIVE OTHERS THE GIFT OF TIME

As you close the final pages of this book, I hope you and your child are already undertaking a host of entertaining activities together… everything from creating a budget to making their first forays into investment. As your child continues to build their savings, use smart budgeting techniques and apps, and build a diverse investment portfolio, they will be freed of having to work doing things they don't enjoy. As adults, they won't have to worry about paying the bills, working just to survive, or doing things they don't enjoy. They will lead the kind of life that allows them to do things like travel the world, spend quality time with loved ones, and give back to their community. And it's all thanks to you!

I can imagine you are ready to try out all the activities I have shared, and you probably have apps to download, banks to visit, and websites to check out. Before you go, please leave your review of this book if you haven't done so already.

Thanks for helping me enlighten kids on the fundamentals of smart money management. Know that you are helping them embrace a mindset of abundance, one that will benefit them in countless ways in the future!

Scan the QR code below

CONCLUSION

As we wrap up our journey through "*Financial Literacy for Kids, Simplified*," let's revisit the key concepts we've explored. We've navigated the basics of money, understanding its value and the history that brought us from bartering to digital transactions. We've delved into intelligent saving habits and the joy of wise spending and dipped our toes into the world of investing. Along the way, we've emphasized the importance of financial responsibility, guiding young learners with engaging stories, activities, and relatable examples. In summary, we've covered the value of money, saving and budgeting, and the basics of investing.

My vision for this book has always been to empower parents and children with practical financial knowledge. By making financial education enjoyable and integral to everyday family life, we've aimed to turn what might seem like complex topics into fun, accessible lessons. Financial literacy is not just about numbers; it's about life skills that can set the foundation for a secure and prosperous future.

The main lessons to carry forward are clear:

1. Distinguish between needs and wants.
2. Appreciate the value of saving and budgeting.
3. Grasp the basics of investing.

These concepts aren't just theory; they're everyday tools that can help children make informed choices. For instance, when grocery shopping, discuss the difference between needs and wants. By integrating these principles into daily routines, such as setting a weekly budget for groceries, families can foster a culture of responsible money management.

Now, here is a call to action for you:

1. Take the lessons and activities from this book and bring them to life with your children.
2. Encourage open conversations about money matters.
3. Explore financial education resources together as a family.
4. Make setting financial goals and celebrating achievements a shared experience.

These moments of learning and celebration will help solidify the lessons and make financial literacy a natural part of your family's journey.

Remember, financial literacy is a lifelong journey that begins in childhood. Embrace this journey with curiosity and enthusiasm. Nurture a positive money mindset that will serve your children well. With proper guidance, every child can grow into a financially savvy adult.

I want to leave you with this final encouragement. Apply what you've learned here and be proactive in your financial education. The knowledge and skills gained from "*Financial Literacy for Kids, Simplified*" can help you build a secure financial future. Trust in your ability to guide your family on this path. With dedication and practice, you'll see the benefits unfold in your children's confidence and understanding of money.

Thank you for joining me on this educational journey. Your commitment to fostering financial literacy in your family is commendable and greatly appreciated. Teaching and learning these valuable skills require effort and dedication, and I appreciate the time and energy you've invested. Together, we can cultivate a generation of financially savvy individuals ready to take on the world with knowledge, confidence, and a positive attitude toward money.

REFERENCES

18 Fun Money Activities for Kids. (2022, November 10). Acorns Early. https://www.gohenry.com/us/blog/financial-education/18-fun-money-activities-for-kids

5 amazing kids who make a difference. (n.d.). Habitat for Humanity. https://www.habitat.org/stories/5-amazing-kids-who-make-a-difference

Akalanka. (2024, April 17). *Safe online shopping practices for kids*. Kids Safe. https://kidssafe.lk/2024/04/17/safeguarding-children-online-understanding-hackers-tactics-and-ensuring-cyber-safety-2/

Bylund, A. (2023, November 30). *What is blockchain technology?* The Motley Fool. https://www.fool.com/terms/b/blockchain/

Currency for kids: How to explain currency & exchange rates. (2022, December 20). Acorns Early. https://www.gohenry.com/us/blog/financial-education/currency-for-kids-how-to-explain-currency-exchange-rates

Financial knowledge and decision-making skills. (n.d.). Consumer Financial Protection Bureau. https://www.consumerfinance.gov/consumer-tools/educator-tools/youth-financial-education/learn/financial-knowledge-decision-making-skills/

Flanders, C. (n.d.). *"But I want it!" How to teach kids the difference between wants & needs*. https://www.kindercare.com/content-hub/articles/2017/december/teach-difference-wants-and-needs

Flores, E. (2023, September 20). *An effective way to teach kids about the value of money*. Forbes. https://www.forbes.com/sites/edflores/2023/09/20/an-effective-way-to-teach-kids-about-the-value-of-money/

Free online games to make financial literacy fun for kids. (2021, February 8). Programming Librarian. https://programminglibrarian.org/articles/free-online-games-make-financial-literacy-fun-kids

How to Talk to Kids About the Stock Market. (2023, July 23). Acorns Early. https://www.gohenry.com/us/blog/financial-education/how-to-talk-to-kids-about-the-stock-market

Lake, R. (2024, March 18). *10 tips to teach your children to save money*. Investopedia. https://www.investopedia.com/personal-finance/10-tips-teach-your-child-save/

Lodge, M. (2024, April 15). *How to teach your child about cryptocurrency*. Investopedia. https://www.investopedia.com/how-to-teach-your-child-about-cryptocurrency-5224013

Money and finance: History of money. (n.d.). Ducksters. https://www.ducksters.com/money/history_of_money.php

Online games and apps that teach kids about money. (n.d.). Online Games and Apps That Teach Kids About Money. https://dfi.wa.gov/financial-education/educators/online-games-and-apps

Popomanoris, Tom. 2020. "Warren Buffett: This Is the No. 1 Mistake Parents Make When Teaching Kids About Money." CNBC. July 9, 2020.

Quaglio, L. (2024, June 5). *The parent's guide to digital wallets*. Verizon. https://www.verizon.com/about/parenting/parents-guide-digital-wallets-gen-z

Rampton, J. (2023, April 14). *The 12 best finance books for kids to learn money*. Nasdaq. https://www.nasdaq.com/articles/the-12-best-finance-books-for-kids-to-learn-money

Stahle, M. C. T. (2022, January 13). *Teaching kids about money pays off—In finances and relationships, BYU study shows*. News. https://news.byu.edu/intellect/kids-who-learn-money-management-from-parents-do-better-financially-relationally-according-to-new-byu-research

Stevenson, M. (n.d.). *"Lucy's Lemonade Stand"—Free stories online. Create books for kids*. Story Jumper. https://www.storyjumper.com/book/read/78614065/Lucy-s-Lemonade-Stand

Tobel, A. von. (2024, April 2). *8 great resources for teaching kids financial literacy*. Brightly. https://www.readbrightly.com/8-great-resources-for-teaching-kids-financial-literacy/

Untitled. (n.d.). Nasdaq. https://www.nasdaq.com/articles/the-12-best-finance-books-for-kids-to-learn-money

Young, S. (2023, April 25). *How to help kids and teens avoid impulse buying*. Mydoh. https://www.mydoh.ca/learn/blog/lifestyle/how-to-help-kids-and-teens-avoid-impulse-buying/

Ziglin, J. (2021, March 22). Financial lessons—Risk vs. Rewards. *NOLA Family Magazine*. https://nolafamily.com/financial-lessons-risk-vs-rewards/

ABOUT THE AUTHOR

Max Miles is dedicated to imparting financial literacy to children, driven by his own upbringing where, despite his parents' financial acumen, key money principles were not explicitly taught. He realized early on that simple strategies such as budgeting and saving a portion of his earnings could have set him on a path to financial independence much sooner. This realization inspires his mission to help parents lay a solid financial foundation for their children.

In ***Financial Literacy for Kids, Simplified!*** Max endeavors to break down complex financial topics, providing parents with effective tools to teach their children about saving, investing, and budgeting. His unique approach focuses on making money management enjoyable and relatable, ensuring that even young learners can grasp and apply essential financial concepts.

Max's writing is infused with practical advice, engaging narratives, illustrations and interactive elements designed to inspire children on their journey toward financial independence. He believes that, with the right education and support, every child has the potential to achieve a secure and prosperous future. Max is passionate about demystifying financial literacy, making it accessible and entertaining for families everywhere—one story at a time.

Now residing in Kansas City, Missouri, Max cherishes quality time with his young son, enjoys playing online chess, relishes traveling, and indulges in his passion for golf.

www.ingramcontent.com/pod-product-compliance
Lightning Source LLC
LaVergne TN
LVHW090408210926
848480LV00002B/498